About the author:

Carol Rutter was born in California in 1950 and received a BA from the University of California, San Diego. While she was writing her Ph.D at the University of Michigan, Ann Arbor, she was awarded a fellowship for a research year in England. She came on a summer observership with the RSC and has lived here since then, lecturing on Shakespeare in performance at the University of Warwick. She has been a guest lecturer at the National Theatre and elsewhere. Her most recent book, *Documents of the Rose Playhouse*, is a documentary biography of an Elizabethan playhouse, and she is currently working on a sequel to *Clamorous Voices* and on a series of essays that extend that work on Shakespeare's women's roles in performance. She is married to the actor Barrie Rutter; they live with their daughters, Bryony and Rowan, in Warwickshire.

About the editor:

Faith Evans is an editor, agent and critic. Her editions include *The Daughters of Karl Marx: Family Correspondence 1866-98* (1982) and Rebecca West's *Family Memories* (1987), and she translated the work of Madeleine Bourdouxhe, *A Nail, A Rose* (The Women's Press, 1989) and *La Femme de Gilles* (1992). She is a founder member of the Women in Publishing group.

Clamorous Voices
Shakespeare's Women Today

Carol Rutter

with Sinead Cusack, Paola Dionisotti,
Fiona Shaw, Juliet Stevenson
and Harriet Walter

Edited by Faith Evans

First published in Great Britain by The Women's Press Ltd, 1988
A member of the Namara Group
34 Great Sutton Street, London EC1V 0DX

Reprinted 1989, 1991, 1994

British Library Cataloguing-in-Publication Data
Rutter, Carol Chillington
  Clamorous voices:
  I. Drama in English. Shakespeare, William,
  1564-1616. Performances by actresses
  I. Title   II. Evans, Faith
  III. Cusack, Sinead
  792.9'5

ISBN 0 7043 4145 X

Typeset by Contour Typesetters, Southall, Middlesex

Printed and bound in Great Britain by
BPC Hazell Books Ltd
A member of
The British Printing Company Ltd

Contents

Illustrations

Acknowledgements

This book was conceived and delivered in just over five months, an undertaking that could not have been attempted without the help of many more than those whose names appear on the title page.

First thanks must go to Ros de Lanerolle of The Women's Press, for her swift response to the initial idea and her continuing support during the writing and editing. Once the book was commissioned there emerged, in London, Stratford, the University of Warwick and elsewhere, a team of supporters who were always generous with their time and advice. They include Janet Bailey, Elizabeth Britten, Maureen Brown, Edwardine Chillington, Rosie Dewar, Deborah Findlay, John Goode, Miriam Gilbert, Judy Jackson, Brigid Moriaty, Sheila Murphy, Michael Poulton, Emily Ridgard, Elizabeth Rignall, Barrie Rutter, Robert Smallwood, John Stokes and Jenny Whybrow. A special tribute must be given to Bryony and Rowan Rutter for patience beyond their years. We also want to thank Mary White, Marian Pringle and the staff of the Shakespeare Centre Library, Stratford-upon-Avon; the British Academy, who provided a grant to assist with the initial research; and the sixth form of the James Allen School for Girls.

We owe a special debt to Tony Howard, who read drafts of many of the chapters and made valuable suggestions, and to the theatre critics whose reviews have jogged memories: Michael Billington, Michael Coveney, James Fenton and Michael Ratcliffe. Our final thanks go to everyone at The Women's Press for their enthusiasm and hard work, including Kate Hardy, Debbie Licorish, Suzanne Perkins, Lucienne Roberts, Lynne Stevenson and our in-house editor Daphne Tagg, whose intelligence and good humour steered us firmly through the last lap.

Faith Evans
Carol Rutter
August 1988

I will be more jealous of thee than a Barbary cock-pigeon over his hen, more clamorous than a parrot against rain, more new-fangled than an ape, more giddy in my desires than a monkey; I will weep for nothing, like Diana in the fountain . . .
Rosalind, *As You Like It*, IV, i

—————————————————————

Introduction

The clamorous voices of this book belong to Sinead Cusack, Paola Dionisotti, Fiona Shaw, Juliet Stevenson and Harriet Walter, actresses whose work for the Royal Shakespeare Company has spanned a decade and whose professional coming of age has coincided with the rise of the women's movement. They have played most of Shakespeare's major female roles. In rehearsal and in production, they have interrogated their playwright, their directors and their fellow actors, and they have re-examined roles whose reputations seemed settled. Sinead Cusack played a golden, child-like Lady Macbeth; Juliet Stevenson saw a Rosalind who was an iconoclast, assaulting romantic conventions; Fiona Shaw discovered in the silence of Kate, 'the shrew', a voice to challenge her community; Harriet Walter played a Helena who acquired a sense of her own integrity by passing active, 'masculine' tests of virtue. And Paola Dionisotti, with two landmark performances as Kate and Isabella in the 1978 Stratford season, quite unconsciously inaugurated this decade of rediscovery.

These actresses are political, in the widest sense of the word. By redefining Shakespeare's heroines, they have opened up new perspectives on how 'his' women are portrayed on stage. Yet when they talk about this process of recuperation they show a diffidence that is based on a profound mistrust of any definitive interpretation.

There is a sixth voice. It is mine. An academic, married to an actor, I have spent most of my professional life thinking and talking about Shakespeare's plays in performance, and tracking down the Elizabethan players who first performed these roles. Those boy actors cannot tell us what Shakespeare's first Kate made of the character's final speech. But we *can* record how our own actresses have interpreted those lines, and what they've made us understand both about the role and about ourselves.

Clamorous Voices is a contribution to theatre history. It puts on record some of the choices these actresses made in some key productions that were unforgettable not just because they reinterpreted the roles, but because they challenged us to confront ourselves in them – the reason we still go to see these plays is that they continue to inform us who we are.

This book has another purpose too. Increasingly, actresses are being asked to account for their work by those who want to restore

Shakespeare to the theatre, to see plays as scripts for performance and each production as a fresh act of interpretation. Actresses have become the new critics. Standing as I do with a foot in each camp, I share the academic's eagerness to learn from the actress, to consider her an authority on a role she has played night after night, but I sympathise with her reluctance to answer some of the questions that are put to her. Her job is to play the part, not to explain its significance. Besides, shouldn't the performance stand as its own interpretation? What more can the actress be asked to tell us? If we want her to double as commentator, we must learn to ask appropriate questions. This book is a first venture in that direction, prompted by women who have taught me to ask 'how' and 'what' but almost never 'why'; whose performances have stimulated and excited audiences, but disturbed them as well. In the largest sense of the word, these actresses are political; they have helped redefine how women are portrayed on the stage, and they have shaped how our decade sees Shakespeare's roles.

I had seen most of their performances. I also knew snatches of biography: how they had arrived at the RSC, where their breaks had come. As the book developed I came to see how the crisscrossing of their professional lives had linked them in a network of influence and collaboration (making nonsense, as they were quick to point out, of an early editorial decision to refer to them by their surnames). They have played opposite each other, inherited roles from each other, shared dressing rooms, leading men, directors and designers. They have tutored and challenged each other, and occasionally stretched each other's performances. Some are close friends. Three are RSC Associate Artists (a largely honorific distinction that nevertheless identifies a corps of actors who return to the RSC season after season).

Only Sinead Cusack comes from a theatrical background. Her mother and father met on stage. Her sisters are actresses. She is married to an actor. Her son, too, has performed at Stratford. She was born in 1948 and began acting as a child in Ireland, moving on to ingénue roles at the Abbey Theatre, Dublin. She came to the RSC 'through the back door' – her phrase – taking over in plays already running in the repertoire. Terry Hands eventually invited her to play Celia in 1980, and after her triumph as Beatrice in Hands' production of *Much Ado About Nothing* (1983) she became an Associate Artist. Sinead has the widest range of Shakespearean roles to her credit: Portia, Isabella, Lady Anne, Kate, Celia, Beatrice, Olivia, Rosaline, Juliet, Desdemona, Lady Macbeth. She thinks she might be able to 'get away with Cleopatra in about ten years' time'. Sinead describes her acting as 'a shy person's revenge upon the world'.

Paola Dionisotti spent only that single landmark season in Stratford and London with the RSC; she has not been back to Stratford since 1979. Born in Turin in 1946, the daughter of a teacher and an eminent Italian historian, she trained at the Drama Centre, London, from 1964 to 1967 and came to the RSC in 1978 via radical repertory companies and the fringe. Since then she has worked primarily in mainstream theatre, including the National, the Chichester Festival and the Greenwich Theatre, but she continues to feel that some of the most exciting work being done today springs from alternative companies, many of which, she laments, are no longer based in England. 'I want a theatre that is in touch with the life around it. And I want an audience that is brave and demanding.' It is craft rather than glamour that attracts her to the profession: 'I see myself as a jobbing actress.' Her heightened awareness of technique – a product of her training – has made her work a continual source of encouragement to younger actresses, giving them, as one of them puts it, 'courage to be ourselves'.

Fiona Shaw, born in 1958, is the youngest of the group, but she has already chalked up an impressive list of credits: Portia, Beatrice, Kate, Celia, Rosaline, as well as parts in plays by Ben Jonson, Sheridan, Gorky and Howard Brenton. The daughter of an eye surgeon, she read philosophy at Cork University, went to the Royal Academy of Dramatic Art, then to Bolton to play Rosaline in *Love's Labours Lost.* The role of Julia in the National Theatre production of *The Rivals* (1983) established her with audiences and critics alike as a dazzling comedienne. The following year the RSC cast her as Celia to Juliet Stevenson's Rosalind in *As You Like It.* She played Mary Stuart opposite Paola's Elizabeth I in Schiller's *Mary Stuart* (1988) and, with Harriet Walter, was a member of the 1987–8 RSC season. Fiona sees herself as an actress who 'likes the challenge of difficult parts'.

Juliet Stevenson, born in 1956, comes from an army family. After training at RADA, she toured with the Theatre Centre, performing plays for children. It was accident that took her to Stratford: an actress tore a muscle and within hours Juliet found herself on a train bound for the RSC. That first season, 1978–9, she played an assortment of small parts: a hell-hound and strange shape in *The Tempest,* Curtis – a man's role – in Paola's *Shrew,* and third nun/whore in *Measure for Measure.* Later she moved up to play Lady Percy in the touring version of *Henry IV* (1980) and Titania/Hippolyta in *A Midsummer Night's Dream* (1981); Harriet Walter was Helena. Two years later, as Isabella, she won wide acclaim in *Measure for Measure.* Since then she has extended her range with Rosalind, Cressida, Madame de Tourvelle in *Les Liaisons Dangereuses* and the lead in Lorca's *Yerma* at the National Theatre. She was made an RSC Associate Artist in 1986. Juliet describes herself as an actress who is chiefly interested in 'clearing away the rubble of tradition that threatens to bury the roles, but the play – the whole play, not just the roles – is the abiding interest.'

Harriet Walter thinks of acting as 'what I do with who I am'. Born in 1950 and educated at a girls' boarding school, she decided that she wanted to be an actress when she was nine. A trip to South Africa on a drama tour when she was eighteen brought about a political conversion which meant that 'the world could never look the same again.' She trained at the London Academy of Music and Dramatic Art, then set out to try to be a 'politically effective performer' in companies like Common Stock and 7:84. After playing in William Gaskill's *The Ragged-Trousered Philanthropists* with Joint Stock, she made a 'gentle transition' from fringe to centre as Ophelia opposite Jonathan Pryce's Hamlet at the Royal Court. Within a year she found herself in the RSC: 'I was not conscious of any dramatic them-and-us divide which I'd been led to suspect might exist between the committed political fringe and the frivolous, careerist establishment. Rather I made vital and stimulating contact with other actors who, like me, treat every area of their work with seriousness, who question the structures they work under, and who wish to reconcile their personal and political lives, finding in the universality of Shakespeare's plays a potent vehicle for the expression of their ideas.' Harriet too is an Associate Artist.

As a group these actresses share certain characteristics. They are fiercely intelligent, they laugh a great deal, they can be witheringly self-critical, and they are all 'watchful' – Sinead's word – for the women in the plays. They don't constitute a 'school' or a 'movement', but, as Juliet explains,

each of us has been influenced by the women's movement in varying ways and to different degrees, and we've allowed that influence to inform our choices on the stage. We haven't sprung from nowhere: there's always been a tradition of actresses in this country who questioned the received ideas about Shakespeare's women and who brought their own sense of female integrity to the roles (Peggy Ashcroft more than any). But those were individuals making personal choices. What has happened in the past ten to fifteen years is that the women's movement has come up alongside, as it were, to provide a conscious framework for those instincts – a framework that has structured those possibilities of re-examination, not just for actresses but for audiences too. Our 'tradition' needs to acknowledge its legacy from Peggy Ashcroft, Judi Dench, Vanessa Redgrave, Irene Worth, Glenda Jackson, Janet Suzman, Helen Mirren, Jane Lapotaire, Zoë Wanamaker, Charlotte Cornwell, Maggie Steed – and many others.'

All of them, too, are alert to the contradictions inherent in their profession. 'Ours is a bastard art form,' says Paola. 'We are rogues and vagabonds, and theatre should be deeply suspicious of the Establishment, subversive.' Yet they are also preservers of a classical tradition. They have huge egos, but are deeply modest. They claim detachment from their roles but habitually personalise them – 'I, Celia' – translating their lines into their own words. Yet they insist that this is merely a form of shorthand, to reveal tone and intention. Never, they say, do they 'become' the character, yet they all construct past scenarios for their characters and even sometimes imagine their futures.

My brief for *Clamorous Voices* was straightforward, or so I thought. I asked them to talk, sometimes in soliloquy, sometimes in conversation, about the parts they have played in the context of particular RSC productions, all (except *Cymbeline* at The Other Place) main house productions, and all, as it happens, directed by men. I wanted them to follow the journey their character makes through the play, opening up the text to talk about its dynamic possibilities, and responding to what else was happening on stage. I suggested that we might begin with Act I, scene i, line I.

They laughed at me. Did I really imagine that the actress's performance began with her first line? By the time she came to it, a million preliminary decisions had been made, battles fought, ideas rejected, images explored, compromises reached, all of which impinged upon that opening line. We needed to talk first about casting, rehearsals, directors, designers, working methods. Eventually we settled upon the following strategy to manage the material: each chapter would concentrate on the role in performance, while the Introduction would consider the preliminaries. Inevitably the two have overlapped. Paola, for example, in her chapter on *Measure for Measure*, says much on the subject of cutting and casting because the director's decisions in both those areas determined the Isabella she played. We are also aware that the Introduction has had to compress whole conversations and, inevitably, explanatory contexts have been squeezed out.

They wanted to talk first about casting. The facts of economic life in big companies like the RSC and the National mean that casting is often reduced to the mechanical process of matching parts to available actors. But ideally, 'when directors invite a particular actress to take on a role, they are attempting to embody an imaginative concept of a character in the physical properties, voice and gravitas of the actress. That's the theory, anyway,' says Fiona. Harriet admits that actresses 'can be cast for very opportunist reasons. Maybe your name is the right one to have along. Or maybe you have some quality, some ability the director wants to exploit. The actress asks herself a lot of questions about casting and usually she can figure out why a director wanted her in the role: you can either like or dislike the assumption that's been made about you. You can go with it, or you can play against it.'

Sinead sees opportunism and opportunity as two sides of one coin. Casting for her is a reciprocal process of directors using actresses but actresses using directors as well, and it's a relationship open to re-adjustment. 'When Terry [Hands] cast me as Beatrice,' she says, 'what he saw in me was femininity – that's what he cast, that's what he used in his direction of me. But because of who I am, I showed him other areas of the character. A Beatrice who is very angry. A woman who has been damaged by society. I'm always drawn to the areas that hurt in people because that's what makes them funny or cruel or bitter.'

Paola would like directors to pay more attention to the whole company when they are casting rather than to individual actors and actresses, to take into account different working methods.

Juliet wonders why a director casts an actress in a role when he knows she doesn't share his interpretation of some idea that is central to the play. 'It seems that he wants her power on stage but he doesn't want to inquire too closely into where that power comes from. It springs from the integrity of the actress engaging emotionally and intellectually with the role, so how can a director expect her to play a version of a line she doesn't believe?'

Fiona has worked with Jonathan Miller, who has described casting as a blind date between a text and a living person, but she thinks 'there is more to it than that. It's not a blind introduction. The reputation of the actress is already informing the first date. The director knows well enough what he's casting. But it is true that, for the actress, all too frequently casting is a blind date with the *director*.'

Whether they collaborate with a director's view of them or resist it, they do not want to be trapped by type-casting. Fiona, for example, says, 'I adore having fun on stage; I think that's one of my strengths as an actress. But I don't want to be limited by a reputation for playing high comedy.' She regularly turns her career in different directions.

Once they have been cast, they approach a role in various ways. Sinead, who describes herself as an intuitive actress, always starts with something physical. 'For Lady Macbeth I spent some time in a Scottish castle; for Beatrice, I learned to dance. Beatrice has a physical grace which I think is terribly important, so my movements as Beatrice were as fluid as Kate's were jagged. For Kate, I pumped iron.' Fiona had the same instinct about Kate. 'Originally, I had the idea that because Kate didn't have a lot of language, she was very physical. I wanted to do weightlifting.'

Juliet, too, begins with something physical. Before *Measure for Measure* she spent three days in a convent: 'What you're doing is focusing, hoarding experience and observation, sharpening your concentration, gathering sense, memories and images.' Next she works on the text. 'I think that's where you have to start with Shakespeare: the imagery he gives the character, the kind of language, the rhythms. An actress may find improvisation useful after she's done that work on the text, but not before. With Shakespeare, you begin with the words, and you build from there. Your choices are made from the language.' Paola agrees: 'You start with the text. And then if there are any gaps, any things you can't crack, you start asking other questions.'

For many actresses, the rehearsal period – usually six to nine weeks at the RSC – is the most stimulating part of a production, which, with the Stratford and London run, is in practice a two-year commitment. They like the danger and discovery of rehearsals – they use the metaphor of 'journey', and Juliet talks excitedly of 'uncharted territories'.

But the rehearsal room can also sound like a lion's den, where, Fiona says, actresses 'experience a regular crisis':

You are often alone. You are often the only woman in the room. It's an old refrain but it goes on being a relevant state that affects the per-formances we ultimately give. Men don't experience it, so they never have to deal with it. The Kate I played in *The Shrew* was a direct product of the rehearsal process. I was conscious of wanting to radiate the sense of terribly clouded confusion that overwhelms you when you are the only woman around. That was Kate's position, and it was mine: she in that mad marriage, me in rehearsal. Men, together, sometimes speak a funny language. You don't know what's happening, and you get so confused that you can no longer see. You become one frown. I get like that sometimes; so did my Kate.

As they talk about rehearsals it becomes painfully clear that in this medium, art and life sometimes map on to each other so that the actress's journey through the rehearsal comes to take on the emotional resonances of the character's journey through the play. Recollections of rehearsals for *The Shrew* and *Measure for Measure* begin to sound like up-dated synopses of the plots. Paola, who has survived her fair share of traumatic rehearsals, sums it up: 'The story any production tells is not just the story of the play, it's also the story of those actors as they rehearsed it.'

A rehearsal room dominated by men can be threatening in another way: it may endanger the integrity of the role, not by manipulating women into playing out clichéd male notions of the character but by provoking them to the opposite extreme. 'You can easily wind up replacing one kind of distortion with another,' Juliet explains.

Something happens to an actress in a rehearsal room which never happens to an actor. It's something of an identity crisis. If you are interested in how women are portrayed on stage and in re-investigating Shakespeare's women from scratch, you feel a responsibility to the women that does not necessarily go hand in hand with creativity, because you go into the rehearsal room feeling slightly defensive of them. You react against the way tradition and prejudice have stigmatised them – Cressida the whore, Kate the shrew – and every time they're judged you feel protective. Perhaps too protective. So you might end up playing a Cressida who is above reproach and a Kate who's neurotic, not shrewish.

When Juliet played Isabella she was so determined 'to avoid the stereotype that deems her a frigid hysteric that I ignored her sexual ambivalence almost entirely'. Maybe this problem will be solved by time as a new generation of actresses inherits these rehabilitated roles and feels free to play them for their complexities. 'My ideal aim,' says Juliet, 'is to keep on trying to shift perceptions of the characters but to have the courage to explore their contradictions, without censorship, at the same time.'

Not all actresses lament their isolation in the rehearsal room; paradoxically, the presence of a sympathetic fellow actress can sometimes undermine rather than boost confidence. Sinead found this when she was rehearsing *Macbeth*.

My understudy wanted to watch. She was very supportive; she wanted to learn the role. But I found it difficult to make emotional decisions with her there, and in the end I had to ask her not to come any more. It's scary enough anyway, the feeling of nakedness that you have in rehearsals; and I kept thinking that she might have made different choices, might have wanted to explore different avenues. It's a terrible reflection on our profession that I don't feel at all inhibited being in a room full of men; the truth is, I've never known anything else.

Rehearsals are usually dominated by directors: they are the ones who set the pace, style and mood, and control its largest structures, keeping the whole play in sight while the actors focus on scenes or speeches. Harriet thinks that a good director is one who gives actors the physical framework, the physical space for their performance. As she sees it:

The best relationship between actors and directors is a two-way street. Trevor Nunn is a good example of this. He comes to rehearsals with a powerful frame in mind – so powerful, in fact, that I spent some minutes of our first *All's Well* rehearsal wondering what I'd have done if I hadn't agreed with him – but in the initial discussion period he's very open and democratic. He listens to his actors. His great skill is to pick up what every actor is doing and to use it. That has an aspect of manipulation in it, but when actors trust the director's judgement and sensitivity they can allow themselves to be manipulated, and welcome the opportunity to be stretched. Just as good directors have the power to make mediocre actors look good, bad directors have the power to make good actors look bad. The point is that it's their role, not their ability, as director that gives them the power. This is why actors learn to smell a rat immediately if a director can't help them; we test them and decide quickly whether to trust them or not. It's a question of survival.

For Juliet and Sinead, the 'inspired' director is the one who takes the actress to the limit of her performance capacity, then stretches her beyond it. 'Again and again,' says Juliet, 'when I was rehearsing *Measure for Measure* with Adrian Noble, if I found myself bumping up against the parameters of the role, they were of *my* making, not his, and he would be the first to say, "Go further!" He was wonderfully challenging and constantly taught me the confidence and skill to take on that challenge. It was a terrific example of how a director and actress can fire off each other.' Sinead, rehearsing *Much Ado About Nothing* with Terry Hands, remembers balking when he wanted her to play

Beatrice's famous eavesdropping scene 'hiding' behind a transparent perspex panel.

I said, 'I can't just stand there, behind the glass, listening to the girls slander me.' He said, 'Yes you can.' I said, 'I can't! It's leaving me completely exposed to the audience.' 'That's right. That's what we've got to see at that moment: her absolute vulnerability and courage.' I said, 'Do you know the sort of courage it will require to stand there?' He said, 'You can do it.' And I did.

Because, as Harriet says, their own survival depends on directors, they are disparaging about directorial incompetence and the kind of intellectual pretentiousness that makes a director 'cram the area between the text and the performance with "interpretation" and allows it to masquerade as creativity' (Fiona). And they deplore failed nerve. Paola:

It was the day after we'd opened *Measure for Measure*. We'd all read the reviews – some were awful. He came to me in my dressing room and said, 'I think we've gone all wrong with Isabella. I think we should be thinking about' – this glorious royal 'we' from directors once you're in performance, when of course they mean 'you' – 'I think we should be thinking about someone very very young, very innocent . . .' And I remember sitting there thinking, 'We've been rehearsing this show for six weeks, we've had previews, and we've opened, and now he wants me to change the performance radically. Without any rehearsal or any context. Tonight.'

Would things be different if women were directed by women? Increasingly, they will be at the RSC, which seems to be making a commitment to using women directors: in 1987 Deborah Warner was Resident Director; in 1988 Di Trevis was the first woman to direct a main house production since the late Buzz Goodbody in the early 1970s, and Sarah Pia Anderson, Garry Hynes and Deborah Warner directed at the Swan and The Other Place. Still, these appointments are exceptional enough to raise comment. Until it becomes normal to face a woman in the director's chair, Harriet believes that the relationship between actress and female director will be complicated by issues that have as much to do with history and politics as theatre.

As an actress, I want and require a very clear definition of space and role to mark our respective jobs. I don't want any confusion about what the director's job is and what my job is. My experience with women directors has been that some have a tendency to blur the definitions. They depend upon my sisterhood and sometimes consider it a betrayal if I argue with them. This emotional connection puts a difficult burden on the working relationship. It's easier to defy a male director. If a production fails or if he makes a mistake, there's only a slight possibility that his career will be damaged. It's a personal failure, but a limited failure. If a woman's production fails, though, in a sense she has failed for all women directors. It is still the case that every time we do something publicly we are under pressure to represent women, and all the choices we make have to be right because any flaws or failures in a production will be put down to our gender.

Perhaps the issue that concerns actresses most of all in the late 1980s is the spiralling dependence of directors on their designers. Paola talks about the huge main stage at Stratford:

The consensus of thought is that you have to fill that space with very powerful images all the time or you'll lose the audience. It's the culture we live in – the language is TV, pop videos – but theatre endangers itself when it tries to outwit the film industry by dreaming up even more mesmerising images. That's not what theatre is about. Images are only part of it. Theatre began with the word. Yet many directors seem to have very little visual sense, so they are utterly dependent upon their designers, designers who, it turns out, are directing the directors, telling them, 'You've got to create this picture with the performance at this point.' The images become what the play is 'about'. In the 1960s critics talked about 'director's theatre'; in the 1980s, about 'designer's theatre'.

All the actresses feel that in an ideal world design decisions should grow out of the rehearsal process. They contrast 'decorative design', which occupies the eye but does not reveal the play, with 'significant design', which consults a director's interpretation and extends it visually to support the actress's performance and to release the play's verbal imagery. Shakespeare writes a new language for each of his plays; at their best, designers create an appropriate space for that language to occupy the stage.

In practice, though, most design decisions at the RSC are made before the actors begin rehearsing. Juliet explains:

The RSC scenery workshops are so overloaded that the set designs have to be submitted something like three months in advance. That means that the director has had to finish making all the visual design choices before beginning to explore the play with the actors. When the company walks into the rehearsal room, they do not have seven weeks ahead of them and a blank page to fill. They walk into a situation where the parameters have already been decided. They might find themselves, metaphorically, inside a hexagon, a triangle or a square but they won't be able to shift the parameters much. The design is done. If what you discover in rehearsing a scene contradicts the stage picture the designer has created, you have very little room to manoeuvre. It's not just actors who find this frustrating. Directors and designers do too.

Juliet is critical of designs in which the set 'takes on the status of an abstract painting, full of symbolism, but not connected to the human event'. She is wary of dead images. Paola warns against 'images that dominate the text instead of supporting it':

Some directors and designers habitually contrive spectacular theatrical moments that simply collapse when the actors open their mouths. They create productions where what looks worst, and weakest, and least fulfilled, are the actors. I think directors and designers have to be very rigorous in examining the implications of the design decisions they make, and not be seduced into some momentary effect that is going to sabotage the rest of the play.

They all see 'designer's theatre' as a political issue that must be related to the wider context of the materialist society of the late 1980s. Paola also sees it as part of a cyclical pattern in theatre history. As recently as the mid-1970s Terry Hands, working with the designer Abdul Farrah, was creating a theatre that focused on words. He stripped the stage back to the bare walls and exposed the theatre's machinery to full view. This place didn't pretend to be something else. It was a stage. A decade later, in production after production, designers' stage pictures control the play's meaning. 'And let's not be naïve,' says Fiona, 'this has implications for women. Images projected on stage tell us what to think about the women in the play. And about the women in the audience. What is a production saying about Portia if it puts her in blue chiffon and ribbons? How can we take seriously a woman who looks like that?' The design not only trivialises the character, but it hands all the power over to the men in the play.

Actresses grow quite heated on the subject of costume design: a costume, says Paola, is 'a frame to hang a performance on; it's like a cage you can tie bits on to it.' But if it's wrong, it's a straitjacket. And it can compromise their performance. Sinead remembers her costume for *The Shrew*:

I knew it was radically wrong. It was exquisite, but I told Bob Crowley, the designer, that Kate wouldn't wear this dress. Her father might have bought it for her, but she wouldn't please him by wearing it. So I said, 'Let's desecrate it.' I wore boots underneath it. Bob came up to my dressing room, and we had this gorgeous pink silk dress hanging there, and he said, 'Shall I make the first cut?' He took a pair of scissors and he slashed the skirt, then I slashed the skirt. Then it felt right. It was as if Kate had said, 'Sure, I'll wear your dress – just look at it!'

Again, Fiona had the same instinct about Kate, and she has never felt that her gold satin gown tells Kate's story: 'I don't think Kate should be glamorous.'

The costume ought to realise the play's verbal imagery: 'That's what good design is,' says Paola simply. 'It enables the audience to understand the terms on which the action of the play is happening.' A good designer – and Bob Crowley was mentioned repeatedly – 'is someone who listens to actors, who has an immediate sense of what a scene needs' (Sinead).

And a good actor? What makes a good actor? 'Creative thought,' says Juliet, 'linked to the ability to explore and communicate it through craft.' 'The ability to hold the arc of the whole play in mind while making interesting choices in the moment,' says Fiona. 'Generosity and trust,' says Paola.

Juliet picks up the word 'generosity'. 'It's very odd, you know. We have this cultural legacy of actresses supposedly being in competition with each other, but that's very rarely been my experience. I've learnt from other actresses as much as from anyone.' Fiona, too, stresses the generosity that exists between actresses. 'We can be very demanding of each other. Juliet and I were quite tough on each other during the work on *As You Like It*. We're both volatile, intense people, and to begin with I worried that she would be ungenerous. But she was very generous. From day one. Even if she mocked the fact that I was taller than she by calling me "HP Sauce" because there's a line somewhere describing Celia as "low and brown".'

The generosity Juliet displayed she had experienced herself.

'Towards the end of the 1978 season when rehearsals began for *Anthony and Cleopatra* – Glenda Jackson had come to play Cleopatra, Peter Brook was directing – Paola and I were cast as Charmian and Iras. Paola had been playing leads all season. I had had virtually walk on parts. But she moved out of her dressing room – 1A – into mine – 64 – so that I wouldn't feel isolated.'

Negotiating round male actors is sometimes more problematic, especially for strong women, because, as Fiona says, 'the structure of Shakespeare's plays makes us very dependent upon the men.' Juliet elaborates:

If you are playing one of Shakespeare's women, you are by definition in a supporting role. You appear in relationship to the man – as wife, daughter, mother, lover. The man is the motor, the initiator of action; he sets the pace of the play and the woman is usually in a reactive, not an active, position. There are exceptions, like Rosalind: she's the pivot around which *As You Like It* happens. It might be argued that the plays reflect the realities of Elizabethan society or that as a practical playwright Shakespeare was limited by the fact that his women's roles were originally performed by boy players.

Harriet takes up the point.

But those boy players were, after all, apprentices in their craft and some day would be mastercraftsmen, so the company would have had a vested interest in stretching their capabilities to the utmost. Given the range of female roles Shakespeare wrote – there is the challenge of Cleopatra and, in the same play, a part as thankless as Octavia – presumably, like any jobbing playwright, he was writing for the abilities of his company. Across the repertoire I don't see much evidence that less acting ability was demanded of the boys than of the grown men. Shakespeare's verse is as dense and as beautiful, the emotional depth as great, the wit even more brilliant, the psychology as complex in the female characters as in the male. Still, I find it curious to think that as a modern actress my opportunities in the Shakespearean repertoire have been determined by the limitations or excellences of two or three generations of Elizabethan boy players.

Juliet adds, 'Clearly it would be daft to consider actresses of today's

Shakespeare the diminutive "boy players" of the modern profession. Even so, our dependence in many of the plays upon our male counterparts remains inescapable. And that dependence leads us to question the choices those actors make where they have repercussions for us.'

They all have horror stories that they can laugh about now. This one epitomises them: 'He developed a gag that had to do with stepping on the hem of my dress, and it really annoyed me. So one night I flicked the skirt out of the way before he could step on it. His reaction was unbelievable! He threw a tantrum – the rest of the scene went out the window. He just stopped playing it!' Even from a position of reaction, though, Fiona points out that a woman can control a scene that a man is ostensibly driving: 'It's amazing how you can inform a speech by your reaction to it.' Reactions are frequently as eloquent in Shakespeare as actions; silence may speak loudest of all on his stage.

Do actresses chafe at a structural subordination in Shakespeare's plays that they can do nothing about? 'You have to accept the conditions of the classical repertoire if that's what you want to play,' says Fiona. They are all aware that Shakespeare's roles for women run out just when today's actress has reached maturity in her craft. 'There are plenty of middle-aged parts for men, but not for women,' says Harriet. 'We can play Juliet in our teens and Margaret in our seventies, and all the great female roles in our thirties, but not much – maybe Cleopatra, Hermione, Volumnia – in our own middle age.' Sinead adds: 'Do you know what I'd really like? To play Juliet again. I'd love to have another go at her because I'm sure I could do it now.' So would Juliet, 'but,' she says, 'I would be laughed off the stage.'

To the suggestion that the female roles Shakespeare has written restrict women Sinead responds, 'That's absolute balderdash. Again and again Shakespeare gives a woman the teaching role in the play and says, "Let her show you the way to react to each other, in love, in mercy." Again and again he makes the woman the wisest, the brightest, the funniest.' Not always, as Fiona found when she played *The Taming of the Shrew.*

There are moments when Kate's story simply isn't tenable, because she doesn't have the lines. For example, when Petruchio says, 'Will you, nill you, I will marry you,' Kate says nothing. How does the actress occupy that silence? Is Kate shocked? Delighted? Angry? Stunned? In later plays, maybe Shakespeare would have given someone some lines there. I am loath to take on Shakespeare's writing. I usually feel that if there's a problem in the play it's us, not him. He's very clear. I really think he writes the plays he wanted to write. Still, for me, there's that silence to interpret . . .

However, she does agree when Sinead says:

The greatness of Shakespeare is that he gives you, with the text, the support to sustain your vision of the role. The women grow and grow, you see areas you didn't even know existed when you started, so you start exploring those and something else emerges, so you have endless avenues to explore. Any actress will find that whatever choice she makes, Shakespeare will help her to construct that interpretation.

'Yes,' says Fiona, 'Rule no.1 about Shakespeare's heroines is that they are *big* – they are larger than life, in that they have so many qualities. Shakespeare offers you so many choices in them!' Given these choices, it is no wonder that the actresses of *Clamorous Voices* consider performance to be a fluid rather than a fixed art, that they talk of 'performances' rather than 'performance', and that they see these performances as constantly subject to change. A production that is 'set' on the opening night plays itself into very different rhythms across a year-long run. Juliet, for one, thinks 'you discover as much about a play in performance as in rehearsal,' while Harriet talks of the 'authority' that comes with playing a role night after night. Paola regrets that she never acted on what the run of her *Shrew* taught her. 'I never allowed myself to play the Kate I discovered in performance – a child in Kate, a prickly, rebellious square in a round hole, who finds Petruchio terribly funny because everything he does violates everything she's been brought up to believe in. It was that journey, the journey into laughter, that I didn't play.' But what one actress doesn't crack, another will. There will be many more Kates. That is the sub-text of *Clamorous Voices*.

The issues these actresses have explored in the roles identify the concerns of their decade; they hear in the plays a persistent interrogation of the forms and the images that structure our daily lives. Paola sees in Petruchio's blunt wooing a potential allegory for contemporary society: 'When I look up and down the street where I live, the number of women who are married to men who hate women is staggering – it's one of the big issues of our society, and it is a story to be told. Our production tried to tell it.' In *As You Like It* Juliet perceives 'romanticism' as a male myth that determines and distorts women's lives: 'Men idealise women and then rewrite history to perpetuate the myths that flatter themselves. But those myths do not reflect women's experience.' Harriet observes that Shakespeare's women are always being tested, put on trial. 'Men constantly wager on a woman's virtue with other men. They test her chastity or obedience as if she herself didn't exist. It's such a pervasive theme: in *Shrew, Winter's Tale, Othello, Much Ado.*' Sinead sees the plays as littered with 'damaged women'; Fiona finds Kate's story 'so painful'. Yet the actresses take this pain on, refusing to be patronised by directors who try to compensate for the pain by turning women into victims. As Juliet says,'That's of no interest to women, watching women being victims. What's interesting is to watch how women collude with what is done to them or how they create it, their part in it. Our active participation in it is much more interesting to explore than our blamelessness, our victimisation. I want women's roles to be as complex in performance as men's, to restore them to their flawed and rounded complexity.'

All of them are sceptical of happy endings. 'What happy endings?' demands Fiona. 'You can't celebrate the outcome for Kate and Bianca. Bianca plays by the rules and loses her soul. Kate breaks the rules and wins – Elizabethan marriage.' And they all see Shakespeare's endings as 'open' rather than 'closed'. That may be a symptom of the decade's irresolution, its scepticism of 'order' as the object of either life or art. Or it may be an expression of restlessness, a sense that to resolve the issues would be to silence the debates. These actresses want audiences to leave the theatre not with answers, but with question marks hanging over their heads.

And with that, finally, *Clamorous Voices* returns to the idea of the provisional. As a group we stress the limitations of our achievement: we have had to talk about roles almost in isolation, separating characters from productions, plots from sub-plots, female journeys from male, and in doing so we have violated a very basic tenet of the theatre: that it is essentially a collaborative process. And the actresses all insist that everything on record here must be read as interpretation, for no single performance is ever definitive. Sinead says it for all of them: 'Be very clear about this. There must be no sanctification of an actor's work.'

Yet if they were ambivalent about preserving their interpretations in print, they were also driven to talk – urgently, compulsively, and in some cases almost endlessly – about this playwright and his roles, about choices they made and rejected, arguments they had with directors that took their understanding another step forward. I thought it would be I who chased them down the stairs of The Women's Press, saying, 'Just one more question!' In fact, it was they who pursued me, clamouring, 'Wait! Wait! There's more to say about this!'

1
Kate: Interpreting the Silence

Surely we're trying to find out at the beginning what we mean by 'shrew'. Supposing we said 'shrew' equals 'noisy one'. Along comes a man to tame the noisy one. And for almost five acts we never hear her speak. *Fiona*

I wanted the play to be about Kate and about a woman instinctively fighting sexism. But I don't really think that's what the play is about. It's not the story of Kate: it's the story of Petruchio. He gets the soliloquies, he gets the moments of change. All the crucial moments of the story for Kate, she's off stage. *Paola*

I think the play is about Kate being liberated. At the end that so-called 'submission' speech is really about how her spirit has been allowed to soar free. *Sinead*

Kate has a very strong watching brief. *Sinead*

Kate has eyes everywhere. *Paola*

I felt very watchful. *Fiona*

The play is a love story. *Paola*

The play is a problem play. *Sinead*

The play really isn't clear enough to deal with the hot area it's handling. It's underwritten and over-endowed. *Fiona*

Three Kates – Paola Dionisotti, Sinead Cusack and Fiona Shaw – talking about *The Taming of the Shrew* agree as often as they disagree, and contradict not just each other but themselves. But they reach consensus on this: the play is full of traps, and there are many *Shrews* inside *The Shrew*.

The story of Petruchio wooing, wedding and finally winning Kate can be played as a romping farce or as social satire, as legitimising the title or interrogating it. It can be dismissed as an apprentice work – perhaps Shakespeare's first play – that bears little relation to his mature comedies, which are structured around female viewpoints. Or perhaps it should be seen as deceptively sophisticated, subverting the conventions of inherited shrew literature. The conventional taming story ends with the unruly woman silenced, but in Shakespeare's version, 'noisy' Kate, silent throughout, is invited at the end to speak; this 'tamed' shrew talks and talks and talks.

Some *Shrews* negotiate an uneasy truce between the clamour of Kate's story and the whimsy of her sister Bianca's, and most use the drunken tinker, Christopher Sly, to frame and fictionalise the story. Sly's function is to tell us that *The Taming of the Shrew* is, after all, only a play, performed for his benefit when he wakes from his stupor.

Directors, all of them male on the main RSC stage, have mapped various routes through the play. In 1978 Michael Bogdanov put *The Shrew* in modern dress and began the action in the audience. A drunk came reeling down the aisle. Shoving aside the usherette, he jumped on to the stage, wrecked the set and then passed out. As the dust settled, men in hunting pinks appeared dragging a dead vixen, which they dumped on his body. The drunk was, of course, Christopher Sly, and when he roared in again on a motorbike Bogdanov's strategy was clear: this *Shrew* was being played as Sly's dream, a male supremacist's fantasy of revenge upon women. The usherette was Paola Dionisotti. She would be Kate to Sly's Petruchio, and the dead vixen would predict the relationship between man and wife. But for Paola, the director's decisions were problematic:

He was very keen that the whole thing was Sly's dream, that Kate was really a figment of Sly's imagination. Which is the kind of statement to which you reply, 'Right, sure, okay,' then you go away thinking, 'How on earth do I act a figment of someone's imagination?' It's the kind of information you wish directors would keep to themselves, because it is of no use to any actor.

She felt that putting the play into modern dress gave her Kate no room to manoeuvre, because in 1978 someone as angry as Kate would have been at the forefront of the women's movement; she certainly wouldn't have behaved as the play requires her to.

Kate has to have a context that the audience can instantly identify as one that represses her, confines her. If what one is watching is someone who represses and confines *herself*, I think one ends up going against what Shakespeare's written. I don't believe he has written a woman who's self-destructive. Mike, our director, wanted to create a wealthy, western European world, with British aristocracy and Italian mafioso imagery thrown in. Now the women in a true mafioso society are often magnificent and powerful but they have terribly clear-cut areas in which they can operate. My tension in the production was that I kept finding myself internalising; I kept wondering why I didn't just get up and go. And it shouldn't be an internal thing. The point is that she *can't*. Kate can't get up and go.

In this production the 'world of the Minolas was monied and cynical', while Petruchio was a 'no-hope outsider who's used by that society to get Kate off their hands'. As Paola observes, 'They were really quite glad to see the back of both of them.'

Jonathan [Pryce] played Petruchio as that kind of classic man who comes strolling into a society bragging like hell; he is terribly competitive because he has this *need* to be accepted, though he never will be. He's an outsider. She's an outsider. And she's a problem. It's an embarrassment for Baptista to have that kind of daughter, a daughter who can run rings round people, and can do it in public. After they're married, Baptista doesn't give a damn how Kate is getting on with Petruchio. She is completely abandoned.'

In the 1982 production Barry Kyle again used Sly as a fictionalising device, opening his production in a cosily realistic Elizabethan Warwickshire at Christmas. This 'real world' disappeared when the taming story began, in a Padua that was disconcertingly fantastic. Sinead Cusack played Kate in a dress she describes as 'Elizabethan Zandra Rhodes'; Petruchio – Alun Armstrong – wore jack boots, and Bianca's suitor Lucentio turned up in a striped blazer and boater. There was a bicycle built for four, a black wedding dress, a water trap and endless invention that came to annoy Sinead:

I think our production was overwritten with images. They were such an inventive company that all of them came up with wonderful ideas, but the mistake we made was that we didn't throw out the dross. We hung on to so much, whereas what we needed to do was to distil the essence of the play and to find its savagery. The invention clouded the production and a lot of the time I felt I was working against the text.

One image, though, she did like: for Bogdanov, Kate's journey had been prefigured by the dead vixen; for Kyle it was predicted by a female falcon, a live haggard. Petruchio brought it on, hooded, for the famous soliloquy in IV, i, 'My falcon now is sharp', which outlines his taming strategy.

Then he would lift the hood and she would shake her bells. The imagery there was very clear and it was very pure, the way he gentled the falcon. What I felt strongly was that the falcon would be free: it was liberating her to a role that she was going to enjoy playing. And that's what I felt Petruchio was doing with Kate.

At the end, these two productions pointed towards very different futures for their Kates: Sinead's was liberated 'from the carapace she'd built to protect herself from the brutal world of men', while Paola's ended up as a casualty of male power games.

Jonathan Miller, in 1987, saw another Kate. He cut Sly, making Kate's world the only world of the play. This meant the audience confronted her story direct, and it allowed a clear presentation of the difficult issues, the domestic politics that are raised by the taming story and Kate's apparent submission. Kate's final speech is only the final articulation of these issues, and the production was designed to make that speech intelligible, to make sense of words like 'hierarchy', 'supremacy', 'duty', 'content'. Miller set the play in Elizabethan dress. And he cast Fiona Shaw as Kate.

I like to believe that I was cast because in the past few years I've become really excited by trouble-shooting. I think it's a difficult role to cast. On the face of it, Kate doesn't seem to drive the play: you have to listen to what other people say about her with really sensitive ears.

I found the play difficult to read, not at all what I was used to. I had come from playing Portia and Beatrice – who on the page are so vibrant: they leap up and all you've got to do is act them – to this rather obscure woman, a woman who's not very witty, or so I thought when I read it, just reactive. A woman who, *when* she speaks, speaks in a kind of merry-go-round language, in jangly rhythms, dum-de-dum-de-dum:

> Iwis it is not half way to her heart.
> But if it were, doubt not her care should be
> To comb your noddle with a three-legged stool,
> And paint your face, and use you like a fool.

Not great stuff! And yet the journey of the play leads Kate from that to this:

> But now I see our lances are but straws,
> Our strength as weak, our weakness past compare,
> That seeming to be most which we indeed least are.

The pure rhythms at the end of the play are so beautiful.

Fiona Shaw describes *The Shrew* as 'a difficult play full of traps', one of which is 'received notions of what Elizabethan expectations of marriage were. I find that very unrevelatory, because in any kind of diachronic relationship between then and now it's so easy to fail to understand what they were about.' And she defends Jonathan Miller against any charge that his interpretation of *The Shrew* 'merely' substantiated Elizabethan attitudes:

The status quo isn't necessarily a dirty word for Miller. He's very challengingly anti-liberal in that way. He's more complicatedly conservative. His feeling about the play historically – he kept on using history, or his notion of history, as a touchstone – was that the mid-Elizabethan period had included such hopelessness in relation to marriage. Men, like Petruchio and Bianca's suitors, did buy women; many women were unhappy, and men were too, and so the expectation of marriage was rather low. But as the middle-class economy changed, so did expectations about marriage. The potential for making marriage pleasant included a duty on the part of the parents to try to make sure that the couple liked each other. That was a big step.

Now Miller says, to substantiate this new view of happy marriage, that there are many Elizabethan portraits of happy, smiling women, and a lot of graves all over Warwickshire – where he thinks the play is really set – with two bodies carved in stone, clearly people devoted in life and in death. He feels that's a real clue: that men and women did resolve the difference in status by making marriages based on mutuality.

But I, like Jane Austen, have a little bias in favour of my own sex. To me those images may be far more indicative of the way women allowed the system to function: by aligning themselves, rather than by mutual alignment, in marriage. The cost of making a marriage work seems to me to be very one-way. Clearly there has been a system at work which modern feminist theory has brought brilliantly to light: a double-think, where men have described the reality and women have conformed to that description of it.

If Jonathan Miller is 'complicatedly conservative', Fiona Shaw is complicatedly radical, but they didn't know this about each other until they met on the rehearsal floor.

We all came as strangers, which was difficult. I'd never worked with Brian Cox – Petruchio – or with Jonathan before. I felt very protective of womankind in relation to the play, and certainly I found myself in rehearsal being watchful.

Jonathan's interest in the play was to make sense of it, and he acknowledged the difficulties by saying that Kate behaves like many children who are unloved. I have a slight problem with that because I don't think Kate is a child. She's a woman, and I think that to make her a child is to underestimate her.

He also didn't think she's a particularly intelligent woman (maybe Shakespeare's heroines sometimes aren't; I've always thought they are) and he thought that she reacts like children do who are unloved: she behaves badly, really younger than she is, like a ten-year-old. Until this man comes, who takes her on. And without beating her up – which is the usual way in productions of *The Shrew* – he very non-violently disorientates her by not accepting anything she says. Jonathan says that's what doctors do with aggressive children. I think he was translating the 'taming' of the shrew into 'therapy', the realignment of the delinquent.

That's a heavy imposition, because once you commit yourself to that statement, you could go a step further and have Petruchio in a white coat.

It took Fiona a year of playing *The Shrew* to 'know the play terribly well and to hear the heartbeat of it', and to be persuaded that Miller's disturbed child was misconceived.

The heartbeat isn't of a quiet, sullen delinquent, but of a woman who's raging. She's everything she's described as. She's a fright. She's a real shrew. She does bang about. I can imagine a Kate who *enjoys* behaving as badly as she does; that in itself is enjoyable. My Kate was very unhappy. She radiates unhappiness, and that's an odd first beat to conjure up. Look at Shakespeare's other heroines and you'll see that, when they come on, they're often in a state of crisis, but they always express themselves in such a way that you can really hear the soul of who they might be were they not in crisis.

Fiona's first entrance as Kate made that crisis explicit. She showed her to be a woman who had no standing in Padua. Shakespeare sets the play in a town among town preoccupations – merchandise, markets and marriage – and town pressures. To have a termagant daughter in Padua is not just a personal misfortune but a public nuisance. Miller's production defined this context: his Padua was both affluent and feudalistic, its high gold-washed walls enclosing a public place where self-exposure was always imminent.

The Shrew is also about upstarts and outsiders, an unruly woman and a subversive suitor who affront decorum and knock Padua off its level footing. Miller's set demonstrated this too. It put Padua on a steep slope, its street a vertiginous rake. Whoever entered Padua came as if over the top of a ha-ha, pitched forward and having to back-pedal to brake a fall.

Into this scene came Baptista Minola with two daughters and two suitors. Except for the numbers, everything was wrong. The suitors were twits, the father a ninny. Both suitors were haggling over Bianca; neither was interested in Kate, but Baptista wouldn't hear their suit, he said, until his unmarriageable elder daughter was off his hands. Bianca, who in this production moved as if on oiled wheels, stood ignored on the sidelines while Baptista was assailed by the suitors. As so often in this play, a scene that seemed to be about a woman turned out to be about the men. In The Shrew, women are marginalised. None more so than Kate.

She finally appeared, behind the rest, self-absorbed, teetering down the steep edge of the steep verge, arms outstretched like a tightrope walker. On one side was High Street Padua, on the other, a sheer drop. This woman was on the brink. While the suitors bickered, Fiona's Kate ranged behind them, flashing her embroidery scissors, gouging initials into the walls and hacking off handfuls of hair.

I wanted to give the effect of a woman mutilating herself like some women in prison do. I wanted to use the scissors to cut my arm – I thought about women in crisis who, far from being aggressive towards other people, are very often aggressive towards themselves. I was going to try to do tattoos, but on the big stage you've got to make choices that are seeable. I have a tendency as an actress to come on and make a strong statement so the audience know who I am and then get on with it. For me in this scene, the point was that Kate doesn't fit the group. Physically she is a misfit.

Is she a shrew? Or has she been made a shrew? Miller was very clear about Kate's case history – from the age of three or whatever.

Her mother may have died in childbirth, with Bianca perhaps; Bianca was always more conformist, Kate always difficult.

After a while, when people are calling you a shrew, you start living the name. If you're told you're ugly, you start acting ugly. Kate has started acting 'shrew', and the reputation gives her an amazing amount of power: she tyrannises everybody, she radiates disapproval, she makes uncontrollable noise, and it's always massively at her own cost. She'll make noise, lose status, but create a stir. So by the time we meet her she is somebody whose identity is linked to her behaviour.

But the problem with expressing any of this is that Kate doesn't have the language, she doesn't have the lines. So you have to hear Kate's silence and to interpret the clues of the silence. I think Shakespeare is making a point of it. This man comes to tame Kate and speaks through the whole play. But surely we're trying to find out at the beginning what we mean by 'shrew'. Supposing we said 'shrew' equals 'noisy one'. Along comes a man to tame the noisy one. And for almost five acts we never hear her speak. The noisy one is not speaking! So we must interpret the silence.

Why is Kate silent? Well, she doesn't *choose* to be silent. She's not let speak. Petruchio deprives her of her usual noise. But of course action is also language, and Kate does have that language. She goes whack, bang, whack! That's language too.

In Kate's opening scene (I, i) she has to endure the sniping comments of Bianca's suitors, but for Fiona it was less the suitors than her father who made Kate wretched.

Baptista is so unkind. He's focused on Bianca all the time. At the end of the scene, he's told her to go in and he's dismissed the suitors. He turns to Kate. In our production we made an acting choice here – Baptista hesitated as if he'd forgotten her name before saying, 'Katherina, you may stay,' meaning, 'You may stay outside in the street.' Kate has to demand her right to go into the house: 'I trust I may go too, may I not?'

It seems to me that when people are as unhappy as Kate they are the voice of something that the whole community should be responsible for. I met a doctor the other day who was talking about dementia in South Africa. When South African whites go loopy their dementia is always about black men coming over their walls and beating them up and killing them. Dementia is a very good mirror of what's going on in the subconscious of a community. There's a corporate identity of which the disturbed individual is but a part.

I'm not removing from Kate the responsibility for behaving as she does, but there's no doubt that she is the voice of pain in the community. You don't go very far off the centre of a community to appear like a maniac. It's not easy to do everything wrong as constantly as Kate does! When you do everything wrong you really aren't happy.

Kate's next scene (II, i) shows both her pain and her anger. It begins with her binding Bianca – she is pumping her sister for information about her suitors – and ends with her being bound to Petruchio.

Shakespeare is showing Kate in action, behaving very badly to her sister. There's no doubt that she's causing pain, and the pain is written in: 'bondmaid', 'slave', 'unbind my hands'. Kate has tied her up! But it also hints at the state that Kate is in. She seems to be spiralling out of control. She's now got to tying up her sister, and in a moment we hear why.

Bianca, either inadvertently or because of the astuteness that siblings often have about each other, says, 'Is it for him' – a suitor – 'you do envy me so?' The point is that Kate does envy her. She doesn't envy *Bianca*, but in that awful nightmare world of lack of clarity – the inability to be outside one's own situation – there are things she envies *about* Bianca, even though she can't stand her. To my mind this scene screams desperation, with its rather dirty-mac desire to hear who Bianca's keen on. This is surely the voice of someone who herself hasn't registered what men are, but senses that her sister has. The scene is humiliating; it must have cost Kate a lot.

Is it also pathetic, given the idiocy of Bianca's suitors? Maybe. But I know a lot of idiots who are also very dangerous men to be with. What we've got to see is the potential of men in a community, and we've got to believe that Kate and Bianca could be married to those men.

The scene shows a Kate who is remarkably different from her sister but who is also significantly interested in marriage.

I'm sure they look different. The text hints at it. People always dress to say something about themselves, and I think Shakespeare intended that polarisation. Bianca wears 'gawds'. She's a decorated creature. And the implication is that Kate isn't. Besides, Bianca is such a good operator. When their father enters, Bianca's not weeping because Kate has hurt her: it's an extra weeping because he's come in. Part of Kate's rage is at the unfairness of it all.

Kate talks a lot about marriage and seems to want to get married, but she wouldn't marry those snot-rags Gremio and Hortensio, Bianca's suitors, and she knows they wouldn't marry her either. But you've got to believe that she's not mad, that she would marry someone who was marriageable.

When Petruchio arrives from Mantua, however, Kate gets a suitor she doesn't anticipate. Petruchio is outrageous, 'mad', he affronts social decorum. His marital objectives are mercenary: 'I come to wive it wealthily in Padua'. But so, too, are the other suitors' – it's Petruchio's bluntness that astonishes everyone. He is a man who speaks half-lines: he has no time, nor words, to waste. He is, they say, 'marvellous froward'. And 'froward', like 'mad', is a word that's been used on Kate in I, i: 'That wench is stark mad or wonderful froward.'

Brian Cox played him grizzled and square, a man who had lived his lines:

> Have I not in my time heard lions roar?
> Have I not heard the sea, puffed up with winds,
> Rage like an angry boar chafed with sweat?
> Have I not heard great ordnance in the field . . .

This was no man to fear 'a woman's tongue'. His manservant Grumio handed him a stiff drink while Baptista hurried off to fetch Kate. But in Miller's production the ominous preliminaries were a joke on the audience's expectations, for the wooing that ensued was no knock-down fight. For all his ruggedness, Petruchio was no bully. And that disconcerted Fiona Shaw.

Originally I had the idea that because Kate herself didn't have a lot of language, she was very physical. I wanted to do weightlifting and so on. I'd planned it that I would make as big a racket physically as I normally make verbally. I would love to have come in and been very difficult for him to handle. People have criticised my Kate for not putting up more of a fight. I'm dying to put up a fight but look at the text – it ain't there!

And Cox, almost in defiance of theatrical tradition, insisted on playing the text straight, a text that in spite of the swagger makes Petruchio gentle, courtly, accommodating. And dominant. As Fiona points out, 'There's more than one way to batter a woman . . .'

Her Kate was shoved through the door into this wooing.

All she sees is a back. She doesn't know how to behave alone with a man, and this is clearly going to be a wooing. But she has never been led to believe that anyone would marry her. This is going to be at best an embarrassing situation and at worst an appalling one. She comes in – and is *talked to* by a man for the first time; that's what disorientates her. Not his violence but his gentleness. He seems to be talking in riddles. He's a bit peculiar, this man. She hasn't heard people talk like that ever!

Indeed, Petruchio's tactics are linguistic rather than physical. His strategy is to subvert language: 'Say that she rail, why then I'll tell her plain/She sings as sweetly as a nightingale.' And he starts with Kate's own name. 'Good morrow, Kate – for that's your name, I hear.' She corrects him: 'They call me Katherine that do talk of me.' But he answers:

> You lie, in faith, for you are called plain Kate,
> And bonny Kate, and sometimes Kate the curst.
> But Kate, the prettiest Kate in Christendom . . .

'You lie' is outrageous: it wipes out her identity. Or it just might be the opening gambit in a mutual process of realigning language that will cancel out labels like 'shrew'. Fiona's Kate was intrigued.

Kate starts enjoying the conversation. They fire off each other, they banter. He doesn't seem appalled by her – that's pretty novel. But then she makes to leave, and he blows it by saying, 'With my tongue in your tail?' I feel that's below the bottom line. She doesn't mind a bit of rude talk, she's up to that, but nobody speaks to her obscenely. She walks down, he apologises, and she wallops him. I think she is really appalled. That slap is the first clue that Kate's behaviour is, ironically, a plea for dignity.

I think that's something of what the play's about. Being a shrew in a community – it's like being a loose woman, people can treat you any way they like. Kate lays herself open to that kind of violation. So she hits him – she gains that one – and instead of breaking her arm or kicking her out, he engages in an exchange that absorbs both of them.

Then he tells her he's going to marry her. And she says nothing. The problem is how to occupy that silence. I think she's stunned. He is doing what all men in that society can do, which is to deprive her of all freedom. Why should a man who talks to someone for five minutes then be able to say, 'And will you, nill you, I will marry you'? All the banter is undermined by that moment.

Nor can Kate have any reply, for Petruchio is controlling and distorting reality through language. He tells Baptista on his return that her ranting 'is for policy'. When Baptista expresses doubts that Petruchio has succeeded with Kate, since she has just sworn to see him 'hanged' rather than marry him, Petruchio mildly assures him:

> 'Tis bargained 'twixt us twain, being alone,
> That she shall still be curst in company.
> I tell you 'tis incredible to believe
> How much she loves me . . .

This is enough for Baptista. He declares the marriage made. But in the next scene (III, ii) he's nonplussed. It is Kate's wedding day and she has been stood up. The whole town is milling about, waving nosegays with less and less enthusiasm.

When Petruchio doesn't turn up for the wedding, it's just cripplingly embarrassing. Nothing has ever been right for Kate, including her wedding day. Even that's wrecked. There are certain expectations in one's life, like your first communion or your wedding, when it's your day and everyone has to dress up for you. For a fellow not to turn up for a wedding is the biggest let-down of all.

Yet her humiliation had the ironic effect of realigning Kate with her community. For the first time she was standing centre stage, surrounded by a Padua sympathetic to her enraged tears, edgy at its own complicity in the débâcle. And when Petruchio did finally appear wearing 'monster' apparel, Padua was offended. The man they had introduced into the community to eliminate their social problem was now humiliating them: he was a 'devil', she a 'lamb'. Fiona feels that Petruchio's costume should be an affront:

It isn't merely comic; Kate ought to see a man dressed like a maniac. Petruchio is undermining the values of her society, and she ought to see that too. His costume should be monstrous, insulting, threatening – and a mirror for Kate to see herself in.

But Fiona wasn't satisfied that it did mirror her appearance, because her own costume was too elegant.

I don't think Kate should be in any way glamorous. I think she should have spit down her front: she's beginning to appear the way people look at her. I couldn't work out the story of my costume. Did Kate choose that gold material, or did someone else? If somebody else did, then I'd probably be wearing what Elizabethan men thought women should wear, and I suspect that would be a rather dull tapestry. That's why I wear my costume with a distaste for it: Kate doesn't fit it. It's not her dress. Petruchio gives her a wedding all right, but at what cost! He violates all her basic expectations.

He doesn't allow her to attend her own bridal dinner. He's in a hurry: 'I must away today.' The company demurs. Then Kate tries: 'Let me entreat you.' Petruchio is 'content'; and Fiona's Kate, mild for the first time in public, was transformed into someone erect, gracious. Until Petruchio adds, 'I am content you shall entreat me stay – / But yet not stay, entreat me how you can.' Kate explodes.

> Do what thou canst, I will not go today,
> No, nor tomorrow – not till I please myself . . .
> For me, I'll not be gone till I please myself.

She issues her own invitation to Padua:

> Gentlemen, forward to the bridal dinner.
> I see a woman may be made a fool
> If she had not a spirit to resist.

Padua starts to snicker, Petruchio appears cowed: 'They shall go forward, Kate, at thy command.' But then he deftly turns the tables on her: 'For my bonny Kate, she must with me.' Brian Cox made the scene ludicrous but dangerous by addressing most of the famous 'goods and chattels' speech not to Kate but to the crowd, who had no intention of seizing his property:

> Nay, look not big, nor stamp, nor stare nor fret,
> I will be master of what is mine own.
> She is my goods, my chattels, she is my house,
> My household stuff, my field, my barn,
> My horse, my ox, my any thing,
> And here she stands. Touch her who ever dare!

Kate got the message. 'They shall not touch thee, Kate!' was both a threat and a promise.

and running off (there's a hint that that should happen in the text because Kate has no time to say anything; they simply exit), Petruchio hands me a *bible*! I flick through this missal, and it dawns on me, this is what I've inherited as an Elizabethan woman. People like Kate who are purely reactive sometimes get a flash of analytic clarity; it's a tough revelation to discover that your protection, the bible, is also your danger – a book telling you you're nothing. Grumio is standing there with a sword to keep back people who aren't coming forward; Petruchio is talking nonsense – 'They shall not touch thee, Kate' – when nobody has tried to help, not even her father.

And that's why I throw the bible down and *choose* to go with Petruchio. It was one of those moments when I had an effect on this production. I think women often do choose destinies that aren't best for them, and I think Kate chooses to go with him. Little does she know what she's in for.

Even Kate's one moment of resistance, 'I see a woman may be made a fool/If she had not a spirit to resist,' is to Fiona's ears more petulant than persuasive.

She's actually saying, 'Nanny, nanny, nanny! You're not going to catch *me* out!' There's a rhythm in it that is slightly less than philosophic.

But if you're not going to be made a fool of, you often make a fool of yourself. So she reaches for her dignity – and once again Petruchio disorientates her. When he says, 'Look not big,' it's absurd because she's not, but the sub-text to it is, 'That's married life and how it's going to be, it's going to be a rough ride all the way.'

Petruchio is having a go at all of them. But he isn't against spirit. He's not daunted by it; he has plenty of it himself. And that's why he likes Kate. And why he takes her away from Padua, from where she's functioned with that social identity 'shrew'.

Petruchio takes her home to Mantua (IV, i), to a house that is like a bizarre hostel, where she is the only woman in the place and she is stripped of all power to tyrannise.

She's not given a chance to restart that old cycle in the new place. For Kate, it becomes a very dangerous play in the second half. The audience are of course delighted with Grumio's story about the appalling journey home – how the horse fell on her, how Petruchio beat Grumio, how she waded through the mire to pluck him off and 'prayed, that never prayed before'.

The possibilities of the homecoming scene are so interesting because this is the point when Kate starts being really tamed. She comes in wrecked from the journey, still in her wedding dress, and what happens next is that her expectations of normal life are totally undermined. She who has been characterised by violence now has to observe what violence really is.

Petruchio at home looks mindlessly violent.

He shouts at the servants, then the next moment tells Kate, 'Relax!' He beats them up and says, 'Nay, Kate, be merry!' It's wonderful! It's a nightmare. Because the tamer is a man who says, 'You want violence? Look at this, what d'you think of this? Bang!' So much so that the only lines Kate speaks in that scene are defending the servant! 'Patience, I pray you, 'twas a fault unwilling.' For the first time she is the one who's tempering. For the first time Petruchio makes contact with her civilisedness.

Is Petruchio really violent, or is it only a ploy?

Petruchio's violence has got to be real *to Kate*, so that we can see who she's dealing with. It puts Petruchio on the line: he's really got to say, 'I know I hit my servant, but I'm doing it to show you something,' so that when he then says, 'Come, I will bring thee to thy bridal chamber,' it's not carry-on-up-your-trousers time, it's this man who beats servants now taking her to bed. I don't want to be earnest about it, but this is the reality of the situation that Kate thinks she is in. And that's marriage.

Petruchio takes her to bed, but not to consummate the marriage. Instead, he makes 'a sermon of continency' to her. Again, the violence is all verbal; again, Kate's expectations are staggered: Petruchio

> rails, and swears, and rates, that she, poor soul,
> Knows not which way to stand, to look, to speak,
> And sits as one new-risen from a dream.

Whether the tactics are verbal or physical, Fiona thinks Petruchio in love is violent to Kate.

Men *are* violent to women. Maybe Shakespeare is showing us the enacted metaphor of being 'violently in love' – you know, 'I love you so much I'm gonna beat you if I see you talking to anybody else.' What's that about? It's possession, it's hunting. You desire something. And you kill it!

But hunting and killing were not what this Petruchio had in mind. When Brian Cox returned on stage to outline his taming strategy, 'My falcon now is sharp,' the soliloquy emerged from an Elizabethan context. To tame a falcon involved a sequence of endurance tests, a 'warring' that was mutual: neither falcon nor falconer ate or slept until they both did. Implicit in the transaction was the belief that a broken falcon is a better bird. But then breaking a falcon might not be an exact model for breaking a wife, so Cox's Petruchio was taking a risk. Underlying the process was the implication that it might not work.

Cox played it over a basin of washing water, his shirt pulled half over his head, his nakedness partly exposed. He looked vulnerable. His appeal, 'He that knows better how to tame a shrew / Now let him speak – 'tis charity to show,' was a *cri de coeur* from an exhausted man at his wits' end.

His bewilderment anticipated Kate's in her next scene (IV, iii). Grumio sat impassively sewing as Kate, now in a white smock, as though her clothes had been confiscated, dragged from surface to surface looking for somewhere to curl up, but someone always prodded her back into alertness.

She hasn't been allowed to sleep, and she's dizzy. The rhythms, the pressure of her speech, seem to be awake; it's that kind of vibrant exhaustion where you're trying to keep your head awake, and you're almost hyperactive, you're so tired.

And now for the first time we hear her view of things. It's her first long speech, the nearest thing to a soliloquy in the play for her. She is saying, 'I have no idea what's happening to me. What's he trying to do? Did he marry me to starve me?' She asks Grumio for food and he plays cat and mouse with her hunger: he takes a kind of sadistic delight in having been given the reins of power for half an hour. But the pace of the game has to be relentless, Kate's got to be dizzy with disorientation, so as Grumio finishes on her Petruchio comes in smiling. 'Darling! I've brought you lunch!' He offers it to her, takes it away, offers it to her, and *makes her thank him*. There's something pornographic about it: 'I thank you, sir.' *He* is teaching her a lesson in politeness!

Then, having said she can eat at last, Petruchio distracts her. He says, 'And now, my honey love,/Will we return unto thy father's house,' and that's wonderful, because she's dying to get out of this madhouse, but when she turns back to her plate the food is gone! And then suddenly a hat's thrust under her nose. They're going home. Petruchio's ordered new clothes. So in comes the hat, in comes the haberdasher. Speed, speed, speed. Look at the hat, a great hat, a wonderful hat. It's the hat Petruchio has ordered, but he says 'terrible hat', 'frightful hat', and she says, 'It's a wonderful hat!' She is crossing him – rightfully, because it *is* a nice hat! It's a hat of the times, it's a hat for her, a lady's hat so it's not his place to . . . and they're back into a rigmarole again. It's very dizzy – until she reaches a point where she must speak . She's got to elbow the room, to break the frenzy of what we sense has been about twelve hours of complete nightmare, and say something that she hadn't even intended to say, which is that she can't spend her life not speaking:

> Why sir, I trust I may have leave to speak,
> And speak I will. I am no child, no babe.
> Your betters have endured me say my mind,
> And if you cannot, best you stop your ears.
> My tongue will tell the anger of my heart,
> Or else my heart concealing it will break,
> And rather than it shall, I will be free
> Even to the uttermost, as I please, in words.

It's a beautiful speech. The metre is utterly regular, implacable. She's tried everything. She's tried not speaking. She's tried understanding. And now she's saying, 'I'm furious, and if I can't let my fury out, my heart might break, "And rather than it shall, I will be *free* . . . in *words*." ' She's claiming language. And if that's shrewish, that's shrewish. But she can't keep in what she feels.

Now that's a *natural* disposition, and that's what interests me about the Elizabethan model. She's a voice. Every now and again there's a character who really isn't Shakespeare's most interesting heroine but who nevertheless says something of primary importance, which is that part of the problem of our whole society is that women have been *told* they may not speak. And every now and again there's a victim of that who says, 'I can't manipulate my way around it: I am *by nature* a speaker. We've been born with these things – legs, arms, voices – and we've got to use them.'

But Petruchio's response to her plea is: 'Why, thou say'st true – it is a paltry cap.'

That's outrageous. Outrageous! It takes your breath away. He trivialises her. Wipes her out. Which I think should resonate, because people do it all the time. And it's a plumb line in the play. Petruchio has pushed it too far.

He has made her a cipher, and the scene proceeded to make her a tailor's dummy. Dismissing the haberdasher, Petruchio summoned the tailor. Kate was hoisted on to what might have been a scaffold or a pedestal and folded into yet another version of a dress she would not wear. 'What's this?' Petruchio bellowed, 'A sleeve?' It came away in his hand, and Kate looked as though she was being dismembered. The violence to the dress summarised all the violence in the play; and when the men began arguing among themselves Kate stood on her pedestal, silent, ignored, watching another demonstration of her own style of behaviour.

The reversal of expectation was as devastating as on her wedding day. The tailor might have been dressing her for a triumphant homecoming; instead, Petruchio had stripped her to her smock – a gown of humility perhaps, except that it had been dirtied by the manhandling.

We really are reaching the bottom line now. We're down to granite. Petruchio has brought things to chaos. The tailor, a servant, is humiliated, and that's wrong. The tailor doesn't know it's a game. And anyway, it's not right that servants should be abused. Petruchio abuses a servant to teach her that the abuse of servants isn't right. It's a mock scene that uses real abuse.

Kate smiled wryly, pulled off her wedding ring, peered through it, and fixed it back on to her finger. When the stage cleared, Petruchio sat down beside her and talked to her unresponding back.

> Well, come my Kate, we will unto your father's
> Even in these honest mean habiliments.
> Our purses shall be proud, our garments poor,
> For 'tis the mind that makes the body rich . . .

He went on talking until she began to listen. And one of the things she heard was that he would take risks on her.

> What, is the jay more precious than the lark
> Because his feathers are more beautiful? . . .
> Oh no, good Kate, neither art thou the worse
> For this poor furniture and mean array.
> If thou account'st it shame, lay it on me.

Petruchio's nonsense is puckered by a wonderful clarity. And that, presumably, is what cumulatively clicks with Kate. She still doesn't know what he's on about, but eventually the whole lot will make sense! Ripping the gown has a point: Petruchio is saying, outsides don't matter, names don't matter, because ''tis the mind that makes the body rich.' That's a huge statement! And if you're reproached, 'Lay it on me,' that's a huge risk!

But then, at the end of the tailor scene, Petruchio hits her with a new low. He says it's seven o'clock. Kate frowns. She knows it's two. Petruchio says, 'It shall be what o'clock I say it is.'

God, what a line! Shakespeare is sailing so close to the wind. The line looks like a stamp of approval for male dominance – 'Whatever I say goes!' – but I don't think it is. I hope it's not. I think Petruchio is playing another of those word games that haven't yet quite clicked with Kate. Understandably, she is blind to the freeing possibilities of conceding anything, having become a barnacled custodian of reaction. Petruchio's line is really about language, and about how language works. Once again he's trying to show her names don't matter, *externals* don't matter. Essentials do.

It is not until the next scene (IV, v) that Kate finally does see. They are on their way home to Padua. Kate still has on her wrecked wedding dress, walking not riding, and they stop for a rest in the middle of nowhere. Petruchio looks up at the sun, and calls it the moon.

You can understand Kate hanging on to one of the few things she can be sure of. She can't resist saying, 'The moon? The sun! It is not moonlight now.' And his response is, 'If that's what you think, we're going home.' Stalemate. And then someone appeals to her, 'Say as he says, or we shall never go.'

It's a wonderful and an awful moment for Kate. For the first time, the responsibility of that whole group of people is in her hands. One word from her and they go back. Or one word from her and they go forward. Her dilemma is that she can control the situation, but only by seeming to lose control over her own sense of reality: she has to call the sun the moon. But then what she recognises at that point is that instead of always saying 'no', she can try 'yes' – she may as well, she's got nothing to lose. Try saying, 'Yes, I'll call the sun the moon, because it doesn't matter.' 'Yes' matters, names don't.

It's freedom. It's power. And it's a wicked, terrible play because she's got to render herself up before she gains herself. In losing her life she wins it. What a dilemma. What a gamble.

The scene isn't about humiliation. Or about Kate falling in love with Petruchio. It's about a third thing. It's about being given a chance, for the first time in her life – like Helen Keller working out what water was when she could neither hear nor see, finally making the connection, when her nanny took her arm and said, 'Water, water,' that the sound she was being made to say linked to something else. This man who has seemed to be her tormentor has given her, or has allowed her to take, the step that will save the rest of her life.

That's why it's so wrong if the play is about dominance and a broken spirit. It's about someone on the brink – you recall that first image, a woman on the brink – who found a way of saying 'yes' without being compromised. At the end of the play, Kate wins. She can say anything now and she's still Kate. Interestingly enough, every night the audience is silent at that moment.

There are, it seems, moments that belong so essentially to the play that they transcend whatever interpretation actor, designer or director imposes on them. For Sinead and Paola too, this scene was an epiphany that transformed both Kate and the play. 'Just listen to her!' says Paola:

> Forward, I pray, since we have come so far,
> And be it moon, or sun, or what you please.
> And if you please to call it a rush-candle,
> Henceforth I vow it shall be so for me.

She's saying, 'I can go further in this game than you.' She's on top of the language. It's absolutely balanced. And then they have that exchange:

Petruchio I say it is the moon.
Katharina   I know it is the moon.
Petruchio Nay, then you lie. It is the blessèd sun.
Katharina Then, God be bless'd, it is the blessèd sun.
              But sun it is not, when you say it is not,
              And the moon changes even as your mind . . .

Kate picks up all those images of sun and moon and intensifies them. She *dances* with it. The beauty of the speech becomes like an escape from the situation. The images are warm and the meshing of the lines gives the feeling that they're writing a love poem together, or playing a game. She has finally discovered that it *is* a game, and that they can play it together.

As Kate and Petruchio arrive back in town, Padua is in uproar. Strangers are pounding on doors and being refused admittance. Servants are pretending to be their masters, and Bianca has eloped with what everybody thinks is her tutor. Kate watches from the sidelines as the outrageous discovery is made. But whatever triumph she may feel at seeing Bianca transformed into a black sheep she caps in the final act by the coup she pulls off at Bianca's wedding dinner.

Jonathan Miller set it as a street party. A huge table loaded with bread and fruit straddled the stage, and everyone was there, even the tailor and the haberdasher. Fiona Shaw thinks that when Kate and Petruchio come in they ought to look exhausted.

She should be in her muddy wrecked wedding dress. One look at them and everybody ought to think, 'Wooo, it's been the disaster we thought it was going to be!' And she should have the hat – the hat they rowed over . . . They're muddy; that should be shaming, but now she knows who she is. She burns from within.

The scene around the trestle table was solemn, celebratory – until male jibes began elbowing their way around it. Bianca stalked out; Kate followed.

It's important that the women don't separate. In a minute she makes a statement, not on behalf of how great men are, but on behalf of our inability to change things. And that speech is going to take on board what she sees here: yet another table of men making noise. The men – as soon as the women have gone, the men behave like men do: they start betting on women.

Each of the newly married men lays a wager on his wife: that she will obey his summons to return to the table. And Kate wins the wager. More than that, she is invited to instruct the fractious wives in obedience.

So what is Kate's final speech about?

Sinead Cusack saw it as a declaration of independence.

At the end of the play I was determined that Kate and Petruchio were rebels and would remain rebels for ever, so her speech was not predictable. Having invited her to speak, he couldn't know what form her rebellion was going to take. He was very shaky indeed in the scene, not knowing what was coming. This so-called 'submission' speech isn't a submission speech at all: it's a speech about how her spirit has been allowed to soar free. She is not attached to him. He hasn't laid down the rules for her, she has made her own rules, and what he's managed to do is to allow her to have her own vision. It *happens* that her vision coincides with his. There's a privately shared joke in the speech. And irony. And some blackness. The play is dark, savage sometimes. But I enjoyed the last speech. They're going to go on to a very interesting marriage. Petruchio was on his knees. I was standing.

Paola Dionisotti saw it as a statement of utter disillusion.

We came out of the previous scene having kissed. I had called him husband. 'Now pray thee, love, stay,' was an attempt to say, 'We've arrived, we're about to be husband and wife with my family.' I had called him 'love', and that was an attempt to get him to talk to me, *me*, not to that woman he was trying to dominate, but to *me*. And he responded. Suddenly, everything was possible. I used to feel, 'I think I know what game I'm playing. I think it will be all right. I think I can actually enjoy this.'

For Bianca's wedding I'd been to the hairdresser, had my nails done. I was done up to the nines. We were coming from a meal. Bianca's husband Lucentio was slightly pissed – you know that sense of family gatherings. The last scene was set around a huge green baize table. The men were slouched around it drinking brandy, gambling, playing cards. When Bianca got angry – it was her party and they weren't playing her games – I followed her out, so when Petruchio summoned me into what turns out to be the wager scene, I knew something was up.

When I entered, I saw someone quite high, quite flushed, proving something to the blokes. He is playing poker – the outsider is playing poker with the boys – and he's got this huge need to win. So when I come in, he is so triumphant. He's been able to bring me back, doll me up, *and* get me to win the wager for him. When he tells me to 'swinge' Bianca and the widow soundly, I pause, trying to suss out . . . we're part of a game and I want to know what it's about. But the game he is playing is just a traditional macho power game. What I find impossible is, having been through all that stuff over Bianca's elopement, having watched all that rubbish, that 'ado' in the previous scene, I then discover that Petruchio *still* has a need to prove me – just one more test – in front of all of them.

They aren't worth it, Petruchio! We know that. We've *watched* them. But he has a need. He will always have a need. He will always be competitive because he will always feel threatened. So that last speech: he is so chuffed about his triumph that he is more relaxed towards me than probably anywhere in the play, so he listens properly. He makes the mistake of encouraging me to say something. *So I say it all.*

I used to find it very moving – that speech is so full of affection for women. Kate is completely in control of her language in this speech. What she is feeling inside, she deals with and rises above with the language. However desperate her situation, her articulacy never really fails her, which is why it's so wrong that her voice should be strangled – mine often was.

She's talking to different people. To the women she's saying, 'This is what our role is, girls – really explore it; it's like an acting exercise. *Investigate the realities*: thy husband is thy lord. Your life is in his hands.' That's the reality. For many women that's the reality. To Petruchio she's saying, 'Is this what you want? Is this what you're asking me to do? Give us your foot . . . The man I was having gags with in the street, does that man want me to do this? *Who* is it who wants me to do this?' He was triumphant, so he listened; for the first time, he listened properly. And what he heard was somebody saying, 'A woman should lick a man's arse. She should wipe her face under his shoe. Because she loves him. Men are everything. They are our gods. They make all the right decisions' – that, given the history of what's just happened in the play! And she ended up with, 'And I'll do it. Because that's what you want. I'll do it.'

My Kate was kneeling and I reached over to kiss his foot and he gasped, recoiled, jumped back, because somehow he's completely blown it. He's as trapped now by society as she was in the beginning. Somewhere he's an okay guy, but *it's too late*. The last image was of two very lonely people. The lights went down as we left – I following him, the others hardly noticing we'd gone. They'd got down to some hard gambling. They just closed ranks around the green baize table.

For Fiona Shaw, Kate's last speech is about 'a choice that has dignity'. In a curious way, it emerges from the wager itself. Fiona has no illusions about it being an easy speech.

When Petruchio lays a bet on Kate, maybe that's where he renders himself up: he takes a chance on her. She took a chance on him, she rendered herself up in the sun/moon scene. Now *he* takes a chance on her. Even so, the soliloquy seems to go off into a terrible area –

it's a pattern of this play. You think, 'We're lost, we're lost, this is a spirit broken.' And yet it comes back at the point of no return. It starts out directed to those two women – Bianca and the widow – but it's in the presence of all those men. It's not a speech he told her to speak. It's clearly her own language. It's new-minted. Petruchio releases her in some way, and so she does speak. She speaks, and says everything she wants to say, more beautifully than anybody else has said it.

Fiona's Kate was not merely articulating the status quo and falling in line with the patriarchy, she was handing back the challenge of that status quo.

Kate makes the men take themselves on. She is saying, 'I acknowledge the system. I don't think we can change this' – which is a terrible indictment of a system of patriarchy that is so strong it is unchangeable *even for its own good*. To say 'I see . . . Our strength as weak' in front of men is terribly strong. She's saying, 'I concede it. You owe the lot. Feel good about it, boys? Feel good about it? I don't mind whether you feel good about it or not. You *own* the world. Right, the only thing that's left for us women to do is to follow a duty according to the model of our whole society. And our duty to our husband is to "do him ease".'

Kate had been standing alone, mid-stage. Gradually, though, she moved around the table to the corner where Petruchio sat. She sat down next to him, still talking, now to him, as one by one the other men at the table stopped eating and began listening. On 'Place your hands below your husband's foot . . . my hand is ready,' she wiped her hands – it wasn't resignation; she was getting the crumbs off – then offered Petruchio her hand. He clasped it, and shook it, an equal partner in a marriage whose interwined fingers signalled an intelligent peace.

It's the first step towards saying, 'Let our marriage be about marriage first.' And he takes another chance and says, 'Kiss me, Kate.' And she goes another step further and kisses him.

Then Kate and Petruchio walked out of the play, in this production side by side. They abandoned the table of gawpers to their own futures and makeshift exits. For Fiona,

the play lands back in Kate's hands. It's her play at the end. It's a very serious play. It's terribly fundamental, almost transcendental. These two people have to rise, through their pain, above the usual territory of negotiation. They're not down in the mud. 'I'm not slugging you down here. We're going up there. We're going to slug it out on the roof.' But when they get to the roof, they don't have to slug any more. Somehow they've climbed all that way, and now they're skating. It's almost medieval in that – it's like all those journeys of people who go through a terrible ordeal.

What about the other women? What about Bianca at the end? Does she take over where Kate left off?

Not at all. The thing's far more interesting than our desire to unify plays neatly at the end. As Kate symbolises those few who get away, Bianca symbolises the many who stay. And Bianca is in for the fight now. Not that she deserves it. There's no such thing as goodies and baddies in that chaos.

And what about that quirk of English etymology: was Fiona's shrew *shrewd*?

Not at all. Not at all shrewd. She was absolutely, stupidly *raw*. But she's learnt. She seems to go through the valley of men and come out the other side a woman. She has learnt the most brilliant lesson. She's going to be able to handle anything after this.

2
Isabella: Virtue Betrayed?

Nobody likes Isabella. They think she's a prig, that she's running away from the world into the convent because she's frightened of her own sexuality. They won't forgive her for valuing her virginity above Claudio's life. *Juliet*

Isabella should be seen to be in a very strange position. When she's asked to trade her virginity for the life of her brother, she's being asked to redeem a rake. *Paola*

Two Isabellas – Paola Dionisotti and Juliet Stevenson – knew when they were cast that the heroine of *Measure for Measure* was one of Shakespeare's most maligned women, but they themselves found her immediately attractive. 'I always liked her,' says Paola, and Juliet, 'She's wonderful, the most courageous character in the play. She has an awesome sense of integrity.' They see Isabella as a 'role-model for strong women' but they also see her humbled, 'brought by the experience of the play to an understanding of herself and of mercy'.

They admit that Isabella is difficult to play to audiences who no longer share the vocabulary of damnation and grace that is fundamental to the play. 'Our culture worships Life at any price,' says Juliet, 'so the idea that Isabella will let Claudio die for so "small" a thing as her virginity is anathema to a modern audience. Her line, "More than our brother is our chastity," is the trickiest moment of the performance for any actress playing Isabella.' Paola adds, 'Isabella speaks the line with utter conviction. If you're Isabella, "More than our brother . . ." is *fact*, not opinion.'

The two actresses talk about *Measure for Measure* together because they were both in the same production of it and have remained friends since then. In 1978 Paola was Isabella in Barry Kyle's much criticised production – reviewers called it 'wayward', 'miscast', 'directed by a noodle', and suggested that if Paola's performance showed her 'carrying out the director's orders . . . she should contemplate industrial action'. Juliet had a walk-on double part, third nun/whore, and plenty of time to watch. She returned to Stratford five years later with her own Isabella: 'But mine was informed by Paola's and by her experience of the play.'

To talk about the role the actresses start with the play, for as Paola points out, 'Isabella doesn't enter until scene iv, and by then everything is established.' Three men have made three extreme decisions that determine Isabella's context. In scene i, the Duke, offering no explanation, abandons Vienna to his deputy Angelo. In scene ii, Angelo has Isabella's brother Claudio arrested on a charge of fornication, punishable by death. Claudio sends his libertine friend Lucio to Isabella who, that same day, is entering a convent, to persuade her to intercede with Angelo. In scene iii the Duke explains himself, but only in private and in such a way that his motives grow even less clear.

He has opted out of government, he says, because his city is ungovernable: he has let the law slip so long that 'liberty plucks justice by the nose'. Anarchy threatens. 'Precise Angelo', a man so cold they say his urine is 'congealed ice', is equipped to clear up this urban crisis: the Duke will leave the job to him. But the Duke doesn't really intend to leave Vienna at all; he's going to take on a disguise that will give him access to the private lives of his subjects: he dresses up as friar. And the subject whose life he is most intent on testing is Angelo. How will he handle authority? Is this 'outward-sainted deputy' all he seems to be?

That, says Paola, is the scenario at the beginnning of scene iv.

The play begins looking like a male-devised power game: the Duke gone, but not gone, incognito; Angelo in authority; Claudio arrested. Vienna in a mess. The law in a shambles. No wonder Isabella wants to get out of the bloody world into a convent! But the moment she gets there, she's hauled back over the threshold into the world of mess and mayhem again. The men have taken all the decisions so far, but Isabella in the fourth scene is made to deal with them. Lucio tells her about Claudio, insists she speak to Angelo, but when she kneels before the 'sainted' deputy, she discovers he's a devil. He will spare Claudio if she will sleep with him. Suddenly the play is about, 'What should Isabella do?'

If she refuses, Claudio will die, but if she agrees, she condemns her own soul to death: fornication, to a novice nun, is mortal sin. Juliet picks up the argument:

It's an extreme choice. All the choices in *Measure for Measure* are extreme.

It seems paradoxical, but I think the play ultimately is about balance, some idea of harmony, the reconciliation of opposites. Ethically, Shakespeare always comes back to the middle ground. Theatrically, though, he comes back having explored the outer reaches, the extremities. As a philosopher Shakespeare may well have been a conservative, but as a playwright he's a radical, and in *Measure* he builds a play out of wonderfully subversive material.

Isabella's first scene (I, iv) might stand as a paradigm for that radicalism.

Consider what Shakespeare sets up. It's one of the biggest days in Isabella's life. She enters the convent, Saint Clare's, the most extreme order possible, real hair-shirt brigade. The door closes behind her. Ten minutes later, the door-bell rings. It's the lecher, Lucio, calling for Isabella!

The tension in this scene lies in the impossible juxtaposition of Lucio and the nuns. Isabella's journey through the play starts off with a herring being slapped across her face.

And it proceeds with a series of impossible juxtapositions: law/licence, convent/brothel, Angelo/Lucio. Juliet sees it as a play that is built on antithesis.

Antithesis is in the language everywhere you look: many of the speeches are constructed around it: nun v. whore, privilege v. restraint, tempter v. tempted. Words and concepts are set in opposition, so are debates and characters. Even the two halves of the play are antithetical: the first half is all abstract debate, all talk, talk, talk; the second is all action. It's like a casuistic tract followed by a Whitehall farce. It's a very clever structure – not at all miscalculated, as many academics have suggested.

And all the way through you've got the clock ticking. Because one man's life is about to be ended unless someone somewhere makes the right decision. All the way through the play there's Claudio's heartbeat, like the pendulum of a clock: 'I've only got twelve hours left, I've only got nine hours left: somebody had better come up with something ...' Which is what humanises the first half and focuses the second half.

Two ideas lie below the surface of these actresses' discussion of the play. The first is betrayal. They see Isabella not as a moral prig but as a woman who has been literally catapulted into a male world. Removed from the female seclusion of the convent and placed inside the male-dominated Court, she is manipulated and betrayed by a succession of men. Angelo's betrayal is obvious, Claudio's more complicated, more insidious, if more forgivable, and the Duke's . . . But can it be said that the Duke betrays Isabella? Paola thinks 'Definitely, yes', Juliet, 'Perhaps', but both think he manipulates her unconscionably, and they find the play's ending disturbing on that account. They consider the possiblity, too, that Isabella's own inherent contradictions give her room to manipulate, even perhaps betray, herself.

The second idea has to do with power. To Isabella's massive cost, the power base shifts in *Measure for Measure* from male to female formulations. What begins as a play about man-made law and order suddenly becomes about female self-sacrifice. The exchange between Isabella and Lucio in the convent states this in a nutshell. 'Alas,' says she, 'what poor ability's in me / To do [Claudio] good.' Lucio rejoins, 'Assay the power you have.' Isabella assumes she is powerless, and in the male forum of audience chambers and courtrooms, of abstract justice and codified bureaucracy, she's right. But Lucio's innuendo gives power another meaning: Isabella's power is personal, physical, sensual, sexual. The forum for female power is a bedroom. And for Paola it is precisely because Isabella refuses to enter the bedroom, to conform to the archetype of self-sacrificing female, that 'she has been punished terribly over the years'.

As Paola and Juliet recall their own routes through *Measure for Measure* they describe the journey in different ways. Paola is much concerned with the craft of acting, and her discussion centres on the practical decisions that shaped the Isabella she played – casting, cutting the script, working methods among fellow actors, director's instructions. Juliet relates some of these practical choices to her Isabella, too, but she is interested in close textual analysis and what it reveals about a character.

Paola began with a director who saw Isabella unsympathetically.

When Barry Kyle first approached me about Isabella he had a very specific view of the part, which he thought I would be able to fulfil, related to somebody who was rather uptight. I have a thin bony face and a small mouth so I could slip into that model for him very easily.

He saw Isabella as somebody who was very repressed, who didn't acknowledge a lot of things about herself, and who was maybe quite old, 'old' meaning forty. She was someone who had *longed* to go into a convent. (That would automatically make her an extremist. We were all pretty busy being promiscuous in 1978. There wasn't an awful lot of sympathy around for chastity.)

Paola consulted personal history to help her flesh out Kyle's arid Isabella.

I knew a lot of nuns. I spent my school holidays going up to the convent for catechism. My memory of nuns was of quite ordinary women. They were very giggly. When there was pleasure or delight, they almost invariably became like little kids – that was just one of the things I held on to when thinking about someone who had wanted to go into a convent for a very long time, but who had not been able to. Then finally, the moment she stepped through the door, she was hauled back out again. It's as though she's fated never really to arrive. And after that, everything moves so fast . . . she never gets back.

Discounting her self-mockery, if Paola was cast because her 'bony face' and 'small mouth' embodied the director's view of Isabella as mean-spirited, it's clear that other casting decisions affected the Isabella she eventually played.

Barry Kyle had this idea that Claudio was a terribly young and innocent boy, just in case the audience would side with Isabella too much. He cast him very young, and moon-faced. For Barry I was very much the older sister. Which is nonsense. Isabella should be in a very strange position, being asked to redeem a rake.

Michael Pennington was cast as the Duke.

Michael is a highly skilled actor who spoke the lines wonderfully from the very first reading, but from my experience of working with him I would call him primarily a 'performer' – that's to say, his decisions are reached independently of interaction with his fellow actors. So at the centre of our *Measure* we had this rhetorical, essentially private performance. I prefer decisions about character to be arrived at through interaction. The text is a well-signposted road we are all travelling on together; we are moving the life of the play forward, not just describing it from the outside.

   Putting me opposite Michael made a split in the central workings of the production inevitable.

   It felt sometimes as if we'd been cast without serious acknowledgement of our very different working methods, which inevitably produced performances that were very different stylistically, springing as they did from different worlds.

She recalls the precise moment when these discrepancies became apparent to her.

We got together for the first run-through. You know how compartmental *Measure* is: you can spend a lot of time rehearsing in near isolation. So this was the first time we'd watched each other's work. And I remember having that moment of panic, I can still remember it clearly. In Rehearsal Room 1. I was watching all the scenes Michael was doing, all the Duke's scenes, and there was something looking over my shoulder that said, '*We're in different shows!*' And then I couldn't worry about it. I trusted that Barry would see it and take care of it. And he never did. In performance, it was very clear that there were tremendously different disciplines going on on stage, which he didn't seem to have been able to bring together.

Another difference got in her way. The play was rehearsed natural-istically, and while Paola herself trained in naturalistic techniques, she didn't think the approach helped her with *Measure*.

Barry had a way of working *around* the script but not through it. He did lots of character research. (Juliet and the other whores were sent upstairs with the assistant director to do endless improvisations on being street-walkers – you know, 'My name is Rosie and my parents died of typhus . . .') And I got very confused because I didn't want to do it at all for *Measure*. I wasn't remotely interested in who Isabella's parents were or whether she was a Caesarean birth or natural birth – or in male versions of those questions. All I wanted to do was work on the text. Because by that point in the season – I'd already been through *The Shrew* – I had become convinced that with Shakespeare you *start with the text*. And then if there are any gaps, any things you can't crack, you start asking all those other questions. Some members of the cast had great fun with improvisations. I found them deeply inhibiting. My imagination just wasn't taking off. I felt I was making a load of arbitrary decisions.

In the end not much of that improvisation found its way into the production, which was spare, set in a black box with doors leading off in all directions, down bureaucratic corridors, perhaps, or into cells. Around the box were observation points: grilles in the walls that whores could peer through, places above from which the action could be watched. The costumes set decadence against reactionary repression: the four courtiers were dressed as flamboyant Cavaliers, Angelo as a Cromwellian puritan. A single apocalyptic motif of a soul burning in flames was echoed on cloak, judgement robe and prison tunic alike, to link judge with judged, courtroom with prison.

Isabella, in this production, arrived at the convent carrying her suitcase. She changed her clothes before re-emerging to face Angelo. Wimpled, hooded and veiled, Paola's Isabella was the most rigorously habited Isabella at Stratford for a decade. The costume showed her austerity: it signalled a habit of mind.

Almost immediately, though, that image began breaking down. The process suggested her increasing ambivalence towards retreat. The hood came back, the sleeves got rolled up, dirt appeared at the hem. The monastic gear never really seemed to fit. Later, when I thought Claudio was dead, I pulled the wimple off. I used to long to get rid of it, it was so restrictive. Pulling it off was needing to breathe, needing to be me, to get back to familiar things. It was a shock, too. A nun should be bald. But I hadn't yet done the whole ceremony, I was only a novice, so there was all that hair, exposed, and the whole idea of the wimple is that women's beauty should be hidden. From then on I began to be much more open. Rolling up the sleeves – I was launching into *doing* things in a big way.

Isabella's costume was a constant reminder that she did not belong to the decadent world of Vienna. But as the costume lost its purity so did she. She didn't want to get her hands dirty, but she had to, or her hands were effectively tied. This meant that the restrictive dress she'd put on to liberate herself from the world was now getting in her way. Still, she never discarded the habit and this led to a very dubious pairing: it was a compromised nun and a fake friar – the incognito Duke – who laid their heads together to plot deception, and later revenge, on Angelo by substituting his spurned fiancée Mariana for Isabella in bed.

So Isabella's costume was a shield that threatened to turn into a straitjacket. Paola thought the costume worked much as Isabella's language did, and that the two were connected.

Isabella is very bright. She knows what words mean. She's innocent, not naïve. When she says, 'What's your pleasure?' she knows 'pleasure' can mean 'sex'. That's not how she meant it, but if it's thrown back at her with that implication – there's always a pause, like a sharp intake of breath because she's so shocked to have been misunderstood – then she blushes, because she knows the implied sense. *Knowing* is what she's having to deal with. I think that's one of the reasons she wants to get out of the world. She doesn't like dealing with that double knowing. She doesn't like it in her brother.

I think she's scared. My Isabella was very frightened of sexuality. My Isabella was going to be a bride of Christ – that costume was actually her wedding dress. As a nun, you marry Christ. He knows everything about you and he's always whatever you want him to be. That's so safe. But of course, marrying Christ is one thing; getting close to another human being is something different, because human bodies touch each other. Another human being touching you is an enormous invasion. Of you. It's an intrusion if you are a private person. Isabella doesn't particularly enjoy being among people. I used to have this physical sensation of just longing to go away. Why? Because people are so complicated to deal with, and you have to deal with all their contradictions, and of course their contradictions force you to look at your own, which is what Claudio does to Isabella.

Claudio points to one of those contradictions when he sends Lucio to spring Isabella from the convent:

> . . . in her youth
> There is a prone and speechless dialect,
> Such as move men; beside, she hath prosperous art
> When she will play with reason and discourse,
> And well she can persuade.

Her rhetorical persuasiveness comes second; what Claudio recommends first is her sensuality, which Isabella seems unconscious of but which her brother is willing to exploit. This is a contradiction that will explode between sister and brother when they meet several scenes later in prison, but by then it will have overwhelmed Angelo who, listening to Isabella speak 'sense' when she pleads for the life of her brother, falls lecherously in love with her: 'My sense breeds with [hers].'

Isabella is stunned by Angelo's proposed trade-off, her body for Claudio's life: it's a total contradiction that Angelo has such urges in him, or that she has such provocations in herself! They are both surprised by sexuality, but when she threatens to expose him, Angelo laughs. 'Who will believe thee, Isabel?'

Alone, she tries to deal with Angelo's hypocrisy and to decide what to do about Claudio. Paola saw her soliloquy at the end of II, iv as an attempt 'to put things straight in her head'.

She starts off saying, would you, *could* you, believe what's just happened? The deputy is a devil. And what can I do about it? But the more emotional Isabella becomes, the more lucid and resolute she becomes:

> To whom should I complain? Did I tell this,
> Who would believe me? O perilous mouths,
> That bear in them one and the selfsame tongue,
> Either of condemnation or approof . . .
> Hooking both right and wrong to th'appetite,
> To follow as it draws. I'll to my brother.

It's not a restless speech. There's no great struggle. It's not a debate between two things, a 'what should I do' speech. She's very direct. I'll go to my brother, and he will understand me, he'll know, he'll feel like I feel. He'd die a hundred times rather than have me go through that:

> had he twenty heads to tender down
> On twenty bloody blocks, he'd yield them up,
> Before his sister should her body stoop
> To such abhorred pollution.
> Then, Isabel, live chaste, and brother die.
> More than our brother is our chastity.

That's pretty straightforward: all those 't' and 'b' sounds are declarative. And that line, 'To such abhorred pollution': metrically it's a short line. Shakespeare's absolutely brilliant! That short line scripts her in a pause. It's a gap of silence. It's as if she has nothing to say after 'pollution'. It's so simple. She'll tell her brother; he'll agree. End of conversation. She's said it all. She stops.

Then she starts again. She considers what happens next. I will live. Chaste. And he will die. Because 'More than our brother is our chastity'. We have to hear the line as Isabella speaks it from her *experience*. And while the size of death is beyond our comprehension, the whole myth, the whole religious thing that Isabella is wrapped up in, literally, because she's wearing that habit, makes death dealable with. And so my job is to go to the prison to prepare Claudio's soul, because he's going into the arms of Christ. And no human being says going to heaven is a bad thing. It's what we long for. That's why Isabella isn't struggling in the speech. She's got no doubts. She speaks those great arcing sentences that seem to spring out of her when she gets things clear in her head.

For Paola, that resolve carried Isabella fearlessly into her next scene (III, i). She entered the prison confident that her brother would be resolute for death. But things got messy, because she had to 'take Claudio on'.

You know how it is when you're very angry about something somebody's done and you argue it out in your head, preparing the script, for when you confront them. But then when you're actually dealing with *them* things get muddled. However strong, clear and just you are about what you're saying, you have to deal *with them*. Their contradictions start getting mixed up with yours. That's what happens in the prison scene.

Paola's Isabella was thrown off balance by what met her in the prison; she forgot the script she had prepared in her head and she never recovered.

When I came into the prison, Claudio looked absolutely dreadful, which always used to throw me, and made me very angry about Angelo doing that to my brother. Which is why Angelo comes so quickly into the conversation. She almost immediately talks about 'Lord Angelo, having affairs to heaven'. It's like the emotional whiplash: that man I've just been talking to, that man has done this to my brother – just look what he's done to my . . .

As she focused on Angelo instead of Claudio, her language grew indirect, apparently ingenuous, but in fact twisted under the pressure of Angelo's duplicity.

Things aren't looking so simple now, because she's increasingly having to deal with all the contradictions that are Claudio. Christ's contradictions she knows about and can handle because she can put them in whatever order she wants. But Claudio's – he chooses when and which ones to present her with. She can't control that. She tells him, 'Tomorrow you set on,' but he does not read what she's said, which is, 'You're about to die, prepare yourself because tomorrow you're dying.' He does not say, 'So that's it then. I'm not asking any more questions. Help me prepare myself.' Instead *he asks a question*. And that question is: 'Is there no remedy?'

Knowing that there is one, Isabella begins to talk in riddles that keep Claudio asking more and more questions.

She isn't consciously avoiding answering questions or torturing Claudio deliberately with obliquity. But she didn't expect 'Is there no remedy?' She doesn't intend to lay Angelo's request on Claudio, but Claudio presses the point, and there's no way out then. She can't lie. She can't say, 'No remedy.'

Obviously I don't expect him to *want* to die, but when he doesn't do what I think he's going to, and then when he begins to show a marked resistance to the idea of death, he awakens in me what I end up saying: 'I do fear thee, Claudio.'

Shakespeare structures the tension between them in the rhythm of the lines. There are so many stops and starts in the scene. So many half-lines. So much pressure on each other's speech.

Finally he forces her into revealing Angelo's terms. And Claudio is horrified. He cannot believe Angelo has 'affections in him,/That thus can make him bite the law by th'nose.' But then out of the blue Claudio continues, 'Sure it is no sin,/Or of the deadly seven it is the least.' Isabella is perplexed. 'Which is the least?' she asks. Claudio doesn't answer her; instead he speaks a terrifying image of death, 'to lie in cold obstruction and to rot', that wipes out his stoic resolve to 'be absolute for death' and ends in a primitive howl, 'Sweet sister, let me live!' So 'it' turns out to be fornication, the act Claudio thinks Isabella should willingly commit to save his life. She is appalled by his terror, his perversion: the Christian sacrifices the body to redeem the soul, not the immortal soul to redeem the mortal body. Isabella turns on Claudio: he is a coward, a beast, a 'warpèd slip of wilderness'.

Isabella has a great need to wipe him completely off the slate. I think the journey Isabella goes through in the second half of the scene is a total annihilation of all values. His speech about dying is so deeply irreligious. It *appals* her.

I remember finding that image Isabella used in II, iv so moving – 'O perilous mouths'. It's as though Isabella is seeing words emanating in physical form; she's somebody obsessed with the human mouth out of which these kinds of words can come. Angelo's betrayals. Claudio's betrayals. At the end of the scene with Claudio she's totally devastated. She can't deal with anything any more.

And Paola thinks it is Isabella's sense of desolation that is used to make

Left
The Taming of the Shrew 1978
Paola Dionisotti, Kate
Jonathan Pryce, Petruchio
The wooing scene II, ii

Far left
The Taming of the Shrew 1982
Sinead Cusack, Kate
Alun Armstrong, Petruchio
The wooing scene II, ii

Far left, below
The Taming of the Shrew 1982
Sinead Cusack, Kate
A black wedding dress III, ii

Left
The Taming of the Shrew 1978
Paola Dionisotti, Kate
Waiting for the groom under black umbrellas III, ii

Below
The Taming of the Shrew 1987
Left to right
Bruce Alexander, Tranio
Felicity Dean, Bianca
Fiona Shaw, Kate
Barrie Rutter, Grumio
Brian Cox, Petruchio
Kate's wedding; the groom in 'monster apparel' III, ii

Below
The Taming of the Shrew 1987
Barrie Rutter, Grumio
Fiona Shaw, Kate
The tailor scene IV, iii

Right, above
The Taming of the Shrew 1978
Paola Dionisotti, Kate
Jonathan Pryce, Petruchio
Kate's final speech V, ii

Right, below
The Taming of the Shrew 1987
Brian Cox, Petruchio
Fiona Shaw, Kate
Kate's final speech V, ii

Right
Measure for Measure 1978
Paola Dionisotti, Isabella
Allan Hendrick, Claudio
The prison scene II, i

Below
Measure for Measure 1983
Juliet Stevenson, Isabella
Paul Mooney, Claudio
The prison scene II, i

Above
Measure for Measure 1978
Paola Dionisotti, Isabella
Michael Pennington, Duke/Friar
Inciting Isabella to trick Angelo III, i

Left
Measure for Measure 1983
Juliet Stevenson, Isabella
Daniel Massey, Duke/Friar
Inciting Isabella to trick Angelo III, i

Above
Measure for Measure 1978
Paola Dionisotti, Isabella
Offering Angelo 'the remedy' II, ii

the rest of the scene work, for now things start to move very fast. The Duke/Friar, who's been eavesdropping on this conversation, intervenes. He picks up the plot and offers to Isabella the improbable and, for Paola, indefensible plan to use Mariana to deceive Angelo in bed. Juliet Stevenson sees the Duke indeed proposing a solution but sees him also testing Isabella.

The Duke does all the talking. He has these enormously long speeches that gain her attention and hold it and manipulate it. He picks up on Isabella's desperation, her self-loathing, and he begins to pump anger into her. He picks up her energy, which is negative at that point, and turns it into positive energy. He starts telling her about Mariana, and about the cruelty and injustice with which she was treated by Angelo in the past. And Isabella, collapsed on the floor, begins to respond: 'What corruption in this life, that it will let this man live!' And it's *then* that the Duke introduces his scheme to supplant Isabella with Mariana in Angelo's bed – after he's manipulated her emotionally. But the *way* he has done it offers her a new path: he says in effect, 'Don't go into a tunnel of despair and impotence. *Be angry*. And through channelling the anger, find the energy to act.' The speech is full of such urgency. The Duke is laying her open, putting her on the line. But he's got to be putting himself on the line too.

Paola agrees. She sees the Duke's speech, 'The hand that hath made you fair hath made you good,' as skilfully manipulative.

It's about wanting to see which way Isabella is going to jump. The Duke has got to be deeply suspicious – any irreligious person would be – of Isabella's qualities, as well as being attracted by them. Otherwise he wouldn't be able to put Isabella through what he puts her through. In Act IV he deliberately doesn't tell her that Claudio is alive when she thinks Angelo has already killed him. He can't apologise for playing that trick on her. It's deliberate. It's calculated. He's got to test her through fire. He's a world-wise, world-weary ruler of a decadent court. Shakespeare sets that up. There isn't a women in Vienna the Duke would believe. He doesn't believe Isabella. And he's got the power to test her.

Juliet thinks the Duke would like to have faith in Isabella, 'but he daren't'.

His instincts have been battered. A moral absolutist – Angelo – has just fallen, metaphorically, from the top of Nelson's Column, so the Duke can't take any more chances. He's got no faith any longer. But he has a need to have that faith restored. So he puts her through fire to have his faith confirmed. Not once, but again and again and again. Right up to the point where he gets her to kneel on the floor and beg for the life of the man she thinks has killed her brother *and then* responds, 'Your suit's unprofitable.' He never stops!

Paola never got the chance to play this scene with the emotional contours that she and Juliet think are built into it because her director reorganised the sequence. Instead of having the Duke suggest the Mariana plot straight after Isabella's attack on Claudio, Barry Kyle sent Isabella off stage and ended the prison scene with the Duke consoling Claudio. They exited together and a comic scene intervened before the Duke returned with Isabella.

The interval was looming, and Paola thinks he 'wanted the act to end pointing towards the second act and towards hope and to give the audience a firm grip on the crazy plot the Duke was engineering'. Those practical reasons may have seemed justifiable to the director but for the actress playing Isabella they made the scene unplayable.

The Mariana plot is such a difficult pill to swallow! 'What? Get somebody else to sleep with Angelo when I wouldn't?' For somebody with Isabella's moral standards to agree that some other woman she doesn't even know should do that, in her place, with him, in the middle of the night . . . It's utterly improbable, and Shakespeare builds the scene around that improbability. It will work *if* she is so devastated by what has just happened – that horrendous scene with her brother in which everything is severed and smashed – that she is like putty in the Duke's hands. He is madly constructing some framework, throwing some desperate life-line which, *because* of her desperation, she grabs.

But if she's given any time to go off stage and collect herself or in any way recover, the scene is impossible. The emotional base Shakespeare has prepared for you is destroyed.

Paola tried to make her own sense of it.

The line Michael Pennington took on the scene was to play it like some kind of pixie – 'I've got this little plan up my sleeve.' And it made my part unspeakable, because no person who thought the way

I had told the audience I thought, and the way I believed and behaved, would then have been persuaded by what was going on in that scene. I did *handsprings* trying to make sense of it. Finally, the only way I could play it was to endow the Friar with total paternalism. I constructed a persona who was the experienced man of the church. And since I was quite new to the church, he became my unquestioned authority figure. Except that I was constantly disturbed by the things he was suggesting. Things he was talking about. That meant I had to resign my will to him completely. I was being taken on a journey away from anything I was centred on *by him*. Which is why I finished the scene kissing him. That's what it had come to: he was my magic uncle. He could make things right.

The knock-on effect of treating the Duke as an authority figure was that in Act V her 'father' betrayed her. That final scene is a huge set-piece, a trial in which every character on stage is individually tried. Angelo's deceptions are exposed when the Duke reveals he was the Friar. Mariana pleads for Angelo's life and Isabella too kneels for mercy. Only then is it revealed that Claudio is still alive.

And I looked at the Duke and I was so devastated by what he had done to me that there were some nights when I could hardly speak – which is nonsense! Isabella speaks, and it's not as if every line ends flat. There's movement in her speech. There's energy to it. But what I felt was weariness. It struck me at the end that Isabella is deeply weary. She hasn't even got the strength to say, 'Claudio – how fantastic to see you. You're not dead after all.'

But Paola sees that weariness as a failure in her own performance.

Isabella is a lot stronger than I was. What I never got in the role was her final strength. When I saw Juliet's performance, it was exhilarating because she found Isabella's energy. She was much more married to the text, and the text fed her up into higher and higher energy levels.

Juliet reminds her, though, that she had more of the text to speak. Paola's final speeches were heavily cut, and her Isabella was crippled by it: 'The energy of the language Isabella uses is a reflection of the enormous bank of strength she has in her. If a director deprives her of that language, he deprives her of her strength.'

'Barry Kyle wanted a happy ending,' says Paola. 'Directors often do,' rejoins Juliet.
Paola can't find the happy ending in the text.

The fact that Shakespeare doesn't script Isabella's answer to the Duke's proposal but just leaves it with his line, 'Give me thy hand,' tells me she *doesn't* give him her hand. I think it's quite clear. Shakespeare is leaving an extremely big void there, a figure who goes completely silent and makes no commitment. She doesn't. He asks. But she doesn't. That's what a director should explore, and what I've never seen explored.

Their production ended with the Duke and Isabella left on stage. The Duke bent down to retrieve the robe of justice Angelo had discarded. Then he left it there. She cast a long look at her fallen veil, then let it lie too.
    Five years later, when Juliet Stevenson returned to *Measure for Measure* in 1983, both the political and the theatrical climate had changed. 'Feminist' had made its way into the vocabulary; chastity was being reclaimed as a sexual option; Isabella was ripe for recuperating; and Juliet was ready to take on the challenge.

Characters in Shakespeare's plays have become mythologised, half-buried under a rubble of literary and theatrical tradition, which generates certain preconceptions, particularly moral ones. The women are judged morally far more harshly than the men, and those judgements serve to constrict their parameters as characters. Compare Macbeth with Cressida. Macbeth is a tortured human being with interesting possibilities. Cressida is just a whore. With Isabella, the assumption is that she is fleeing into the convent because she's frightened of her own sexuality. That's a moral judgement.

The iconoclast actress began reconstructing Isabella by re-examining her sexuality.

I had only one instinct about Isabella when I started, which was that she should be looked at not as a frigid hysteric with a big problem about sex, but that we should kick off by exploring the *positive* reasons for entering a convent.
    It's our own contemporary prejudices that see monastic retreat as running away, as somehow negative. But many a nun enters the

convent as a positive choice. Leaving the world may not be fleeing the world, it may be a way of avoiding becoming its slave. By standing back from it, a nun keeps the world in focus, not just for herself but for others. For a believer, monastic retreat allows you to devote all your energies to creating a channel through which good is introduced to the world, by means of prayer, meditation and self-denial. That's what I think Isabella is doing. She provides a focus for Vienna to see itself.

Juliet's Isabella was warm, vivacious, even sensuous.

I think she recognises her own sensuality and the need to apply strict control over it. I don't think she's frightened or surprised by it; she wants to dominate it. Hence her choice of the Saint Clares. The severity of the order is, I think, commensurate with the scale of those latent passions in her, which she feels must be harnessed, controlled.

Interrogating Isabella's sexuality was just the first step in reinterpreting her whole image. But Juliet wanted her Isabella to make discoveries about herself on stage as well as in the rehearsal room, and this meant that certain design decisions were critical.

I was very anxious that the production not be set anywhere in the twentieth century because I think it would be impossible to play *Isabella's play* in a contemporary situation. Not only is there no big deal any longer about giving yourself to someone sexually, but the whole idea of the life of the soul has more or less disappeared from popular culture. Outside of Catholicism, notions of 'perjuring the soul' and 'eternal damnation' have become quaint, and they make Isabella an eccentric. If her decision is not one the audience can identify with positively, they will judge her. This means that the production has got to place the play so that the line 'More than our brother is our chastity' can be spoken with integrity. The production – if its objective is that the audience should recognise Isabella's dilemma as opposed to merely observing her in critical detachment – has to support Isabella. Otherwise the audience will not really be challenged by the play, they'll have been let off the hook.

She rejected the image Paola had worked to such ironic effect, the wimpled and habited Isabella, because

I didn't want the audience to be looking at a nun all night. I wanted to break down what they would invariably have associated with that image. I wanted to say to them, 'Look at this person. *Listen* to this person. Don't judge her from the image. Listen afresh.'

She objects to costumes that stereotype the character: 'The actress, not the dress, should do the acting.' And Isabella is a character who, under the pressure of experience, is constantly changing.

Isabella goes on a massive journey. At certain points, thoughts of the nunnery are a million miles away. She shapes, and continually reshapes, where she's going *through her language*. It's revelatory, not imposed. The visual image can't tell her story, because it's too restrictive. She moves, it doesn't. The costume simply can't keep up with the language.

There ought never to be a sense that Isabella is in fancy dress, because I think one of the points the play is making is that the Duke *is*. He's disguised as a friar, wandering around in the most bizarre of assumed identities, and the ideas the audience must be associating with that costume – about authority, infallibility, omniscience and so on – have got to be more and more ironically exposed, compromised.

Juliet's director and designer agreed with her. Adrian Noble directed the play as an indictment of mankind's self-deception. His Vienna was a 'dark corner' full of Hogarthian rakes and dissolute women in rotting silk. Anachronistically, the prison was an image from the gulag – a low grey concentration camp wall with bald electric lightbulbs glaring down, a sign that hypocrisy is a permanent feature of political life. Isabella made her way through this world dressed like an aristocrat in a full-skirted black gown, rich but sombre. Her arms were covered but her neck was exposed. It was an image that satisfied Juliet's crusade to recuperate Isabella visually. It allowed her to get on with what interested her more: reinvestigating Isabella's language.

I am a bit of a purist about the structure of Shakespeare's language. His metre – that basic ten-syllable iambic pentameter line – his rhythms, his pauses, his punctuation, where he breaks a line mid-way, you have to observe what he's doing with them, not as an end in itself but because they give you so many clues. There is a beat, there is a pulse in the verse that will tell you as much about the character as anything she says.

I believe what I've been taught by Cis Berry, the RSC's voice teacher – that Shakespeare's characters live in the moment they speak. They don't premeditate their soliloquies in the wings and bring them on prepared. They *are* as they speak. An image is chosen, which leads to the next image, each thought to the next, and if you follow the structure of the verse, and yield to it, you will discover the way the character's mind is working towards its conclusion. So the language tells you who the character is moment by moment, word by word. You need not, *should* not, be bound by notions of psychological consistency.

And I've been taught – again, Cis Berry – that language doesn't just have an intellectual meaning. It has a sensual life of sound and energy, which has nothing to do with the literal meaning, but which offers up just as many clues for the actor as to the character's state of mind at the moment of utterance.

Juliet's close reading of Isabella shows her picking up the clues that turn a script into a character. In an almost line-by-line reading of her first interview with Angelo (II, ii) she discovers an 'astonishing' Isabella embedded in the lines.

By then Isabella has already played one scene, I, iv, in the convent with Lucio, and the text there tells you something about the woman who will walk into II, ii. What I found textually interesting about I, iv is how little Isabella has to say. She isn't particularly articulate. Her thinking seems disjointed. She constantly speaks half-lines. She doesn't predict the Isabella who is going to be released into language by the confrontation with Angelo in II, ii.

But in I, iv she did show herself to be a woman whose sense of self-image is quite strong. She makes a point of saying, by the *way* she says something, 'This is who I am.' She shows a horror of being misunderstood, for example, in the opening exchange. 'And have you nuns no farther privileges?' That's interpreted by the nun, Francisca, to mean she desires more liberty, when what she's really saying is that she is seeking more restraint. So when Francisca responds, 'Are not these large enough?' Isabella doesn't immediately reply. Shakespeare writes that as a half-line; the rest of the line is silence, and the actress can use Isabella's silence to show her adjusting to the nun's mistaken impression about her, which has disorientated her.

Disorientation is a big theme in that scene. She's established herself in those first lines – 'I'm this sort of person, I'm into strict restraint' – and then there's that knock on the door and Lucio appears, pulling the moral absolutist rug out from under her.

That scene is also textually very interesting. If you look at Lucio's speech that begins 'This is the point' and run down the words at the end of the lines – state, place, authority, blood, feels, sense, edge, fast, liberty, law, act, life, statute, gone, prayer, business, brother – you could drive a nail into each of those words and the play would be staked out around those issues. Lucio has to do so much talking to make Isabella focus on Claudio's situation. All she can do is speak those hand-wringing half-lines:

> Alas, what poor ability's in me
> To do him good . . .
> My power? Alas, I doubt . . .

But Lucio, with his own brand of wisdom, persuades her to trust to her own potency, and to use it on Angelo.

Lucio pushes her into the interview with Angelo (II, ii). Things do not go smoothly.

Before she even has a chance to get going, two little 'blips' disrupt the interview. Angelo, who's just told the Provost to go, suddenly changes his mind, tells him to 'Stay a little while.' Why? Does he want a witness? Does he want to even up the sides? Isabella comes with Lucio. Or is there something in her physical presence that puts him on guard with himself? They're all possible.

What Angelo has revealed of himself through his text is that he's a precisionist. He speaks clipped sentences broken across half-lines:

> Did I not tell thee, yea? Hadst thou not order?
> Why dost thou ask again?

When Isabella starts off with her little prologue, 'I am a woeful suitor to your honour,' Angelo uses one of those half-lines to interrupt her: 'Well, what's your suit?' It's a big shock to Isabella. She's been measuring out her preamble, as if she'd been rehearsing it (as well you might if you were terrified – that's in the scene too), and he interrupts. He's giving her no space.

So she starts again:

> There is a vice that most I do abhor,
> And most desire should meet the blow of justice,
> For which I would not plead, but that I must,

> For which I must not plead, but that I am
> At war 'twixt will and will not.

Now, that's so revealing! Isabella doesn't start out pleading for Claudio's life, she starts out positioning herself with respect to that word 'vice', as if to establish her credentials, her politics – 'I'm with you on this one, Angelo. I voted for you, Angelo.'

But she's absolutely split in two. 'I hate vice. But I'm here to plead for it; no I'm not here to plead for vice, I'm here to . . . agghhh!' She's pulled between two moving vehicles in the speech. Her quandary is there in all those verbs that keep replacing one another: 'I would not', 'I must', 'I must not', 'I am'. The way 'I am' hangs suspended at the end of the line leaves her dangling over a precipice. 'I am' – what? 'I am – at war . . .' It's quite violent, her language: 'blow', 'abhor', 'war'.

Angelo interrupts her again, again doesn't give her any room to manoeuvre: 'Well: the matter?'

Her answer is very cryptic.

> I have a brother is condemn'd to die.
> I do beseech you, let it be his fault,
> And not my brother.

What she's doing is separating the fault from the man who commits that fault and asking that the fault die and the man live. It's a philosophical quibble – she knows it, and the way she says it exposes all her diffidence. It's as though she's trying to rush the sentence past the judge before he spots its legal flaw – getting in there quick with a load of monosyllables and a weak ending, 'brother', which trails off, as the line does, into silence. I think Isabella knows her argument is weak. She split her advocacy in two in her opening statement, so there's no strength here, there's no counterbalance. 'Die' and 'fault' get all the emphasis, metrically and by their position at the end of the line; 'brother' has no strength at all. He's not strongly placed in the line, poor bloke.

The Provost finishes her line, in a private aside to the audience, which leaves her in the alarming situation of facing silence from Angelo. What he then says restates what she already knows:

> Condemn the fault, and not the actor of it?
> Why, every fault's condemned ere it be done.
> Mine were the very cipher of a function,
> To fine the faults whose fine stands in record,
> And let go by the actor.

She promptly finishes his half-line: she comes in with 'O just, but severe law!' It's as though she can anticipate his verdict.

But really they're playing word games. The whole conversation is functioning around a few words, and the logic of the rhetoric defeats her at this point because on an abstract level Angelo's logic is undeniable. She recognises the justice of what he's saying and the nonsense of what she's said already. In secular law and abstract justice you can't conveniently separate the offence from the offender.

And that's a clue. Isabella is functioning on the level of abstract debate at the moment. The argument isn't personal; it's all very rational. Isabella's centre is very much in her *head* at the beginning of the play – her centre is going to shift, but right now, she's living in her head. And she's complicit in Angelo's locating the argument on that philosophical plane. So, having been defeated in that rhetorical argument about the nature of justice, she goes to leave.

But Lucio won't let her give up. He pushes her back into the scene. He tells her to stop talking and start doing – 'entreat', 'kneel', 'hang'. He thrusts her upon Angelo, 'To him I say!' And there's a huge pause before she comes up with, 'Must he needs die?' Here are the next ten lines.

> *Isabella* Must he needs die?
> *Angelo*   Maiden, no remedy.
> *Isabella* Yes, I do think that you might pardon him,
>   And neither heaven nor man grieve at the mercy.
> *Angelo* I will not do't.
> *Isabella*   But can you if you would?
> *Angelo* Look what I will not, that I cannot do.
> *Isabella* But might you do't, and do the world no wrong,
>   If so your heart were touched with that remorse
>   As mine is to him?

'Maiden, no remedy' releases something in Isabella; her 'yes' answers Angelo's 'no'. It's her first come-back. 'Yes,' she says, 'there is a remedy, you might pardon him.' 'Remedy' suggests 'pardon' suggests 'mercy': the remedy is *mercy*. And 'man', placed midway metrically in the line, has to get two beats: so it has a bit of space around it rhythmically, and the scripted emphasis on the word 'man' serves to pull the argument from *there* – abstracts – to *here* – personalities.

Angelo has been talking legalism and abstraction that has nothing to do with anybody named. Now the argument becomes human, and increasingly personal. Angelo opened with 'There is no remedy', as if it were holy writ inscribed on tablets. But she says, 'There *is* a remedy, *you* could . . .' so he has to counter with '*I* will not . . .' He's forced to commit himself personally. And she's manoeuvred him into that. Now it's between the two of them. She's making progress. She's achieved something. She comes back with 'Can you?', he counters with 'What I will not, that I cannot do,' but she still persists: 'Might you?' They're parrying with verbs, fighting this out with scrupulous variations on the infinitive 'to be'.

It's all about the relationship between power and desire, what I can do and what I want to do. Angelo is saying, 'I am the law. I identify myself with the law. There is no distinction between my intention and my execution of the law. They are not separable.' But she enters the word 'might' into the argument. And that word 'might' prises apart the law and Angelo. 'Might you do't?' *Might* sneaks in between 'will not' and 'cannot'.

'If so your heart were touched with that remorse/As mine is to him': that's the first time the human heart has come into it. So, having forced a sort of crack between Angelo as a human being and the impersonal law he claims to be representing, Isabella proceeds to appeal straight to his humanitarian principles. Not to his head. Not to his convictions. She's taking the focus away from the head and shifting it down to the heart. And it's interesting that she does that because I think, as it plays, you discover that the heart is beginning to function at that moment for her as well. The first half of the scene is a head argument, and somehow, as Lucio spots, she hasn't been engaged with her heart. She's been cold. Now she's warming. She's shifted the focus from abstraction to him as a person, and then from him as a person in his head to him as a person in his heart.

And she introduces that word 'if'. 'If' occurs thousands of times in this play. It's a protagonist in *Measure for Measure*. 'If' takes us into compromise, that muddy territory. But it provides for possibility, for miracle. And it's a qualifier: 'If he were you and you were he', 'If it happened to you'. 'If' is the imaginative means of projecting somebody else's experiences on to yourself. It is a doorway, leading to empathy, identification, recognition.

So Isabella opens up possibility with 'if' but Angelo immediately closes it down again. 'He's sentenced; 'tis too late.' That's a new piece of information, 'He's sentenced.' She has to pause over that, and has the whole of Lucio's line in which to do so. But 'too late' opens up another gap, another come-back.

You know that speech of Leontes' in *The Winter's Tale*, 'Too hot, too hot', when he first gives vent to his jealousy? The rhythm is very staccato, jerky – it's like a car trying to start in the morning. Chonk. Chonk. It's the same sort of rhythm Isabella has here. 'Too late? [Chonk] Why, no [Chonk].' But then the car really begins to get going. She goes rev, rev, rev, and she's away:

> I that do speak a word
> May call it back again. Well, believe this,
> No ceremony that to great ones longs,
> Not the king's crown, nor the deputed sword,
> The marshal's truncheon, nor the judge's robe,
> Become them with one half so good a grace
> As mercy does.

Those last five lines constitute the longest sentence she's spoken so far. It's all one breath. It's unstoppable. It's as though something in that phrase 'too late' has unleashed all this torrent. And Angelo says nothing. Isabella has said it *all*, and Angelo says nothing, so she has to start again. There's a big silence, then she leaps in again:

> If he had been as you and you as he,
> You would have slipped like him; but he, like you,
> Would not have been so stern.

And Angelo says, 'Be gone.'

That's interesting. As soon as she mentions slipping he says, 'Get out.' She's moving in on him very fast. And he doesn't like the argument. She's separated him from the law, from his position as impersonal judge; she's appealed to him as a human being; and now she's aligning him with the actual offender! She doesn't mean 'You would have slipped' as anything more than an axiom of human life: 'You would have slipped because *anyone* in that circumstance would have slipped.' But he's personalising it.

Maybe that word 'slip' triggers in him in the capacity to slip – just as some of his words have triggered things in her. Their language is so erotic. They keep landing right in the middle of each other's line, in the middle of each other's thought. He gives her something, and she lands on it, he lands on that, and she lands on *that*. It's such an interdependent development. They're listening so hard to each other. That's partly what's erotic about it: they're receiving each other.

And each of them seems, perhaps unconsciously, to be arousing and inflaming the other – propelling each other into ever wider and deeper waters. It's like that in II, iv, their next scene, when he puts to her the supposedly theoretical proposition: if somebody wanted you to lay down the treasures of your body, what would you do? Her answer is studied – it follows a long pause after Angelo's half-line – and it's triggered by Angelo's word 'treasures':

> As much for my poor brother as myself:
> That is, were I under terms of death,
> Th' impression of keen whips I'd wear as rubies,
> And strip myself to death as to a bed
> That long I have been sick for, ere I'd yield
> My body up to shame.

Many critics think this speech betrays Isabella's unexamined sensuality. It's so erotic, and they don't think she's aware of the implied sense of the language. (I think she is. The Isabella I played was clued in to her sexuality from the first.) But Isabella habitually takes words other characters have spoken and raises the ante on them – 'privileges', 'remedy', 'forfeit'. The character who introduces the word meant one thing, but the word then triggers explorations of fuller meanings in Isabella. Here, it's Angelo's word 'treasures' that's the trigger. He's used it as a kind of salacious euphemism: 'lay down the treasures of your body' means being laid. But Isabella picks up on 'treasures', *explores* it, makes her body a treasure indeed, through martyrdom, takes the word beyond anything Angelo intended, and so in a way defeats him.

That speech about whips and rubies isn't anything startlingly new. She and Angelo have been copulating across the verse ever since they first met.

But to go back to II, ii, and that word 'slip' she gives him: is it a trigger? Slipping isn't something he can even look at. And he wants her out. He has no come-back to that argument. It's as though he has no mirrors in his house.

But Isabella isn't going to leave. She's on the attack now, taking over his space – I eventually sat in his chair – and he's getting defensive. She's talking power and she's playing power, and that's interesting because she herself is moving away from theological argument into the world, the affairs of worldly office, ceremony, and power. Angelo is no longer the *law*, he's a man who's abusing his power. And when he falls back on that lame abstraction, 'Your brother is a forfeit of the law' – those tablets again – she lands on him with total conviction; she's on home ground now.

Why, all the souls that were were forfeit once,
And He that might the vantage best have took
Found out the remedy. How would you be,
If He, which is the top of judgement, should
But judge you as you are? O think on that,
And mercy then will breathe within your lips,
Like man new made.

She gallops across those first two lines, punches in 'found out', picks up 'remedy' – when he's already said 'no remedy' – then knocks out four strong monosyllables, 'How would you be'. 'Forfeit' is the key word here. Angelo used it as a petty legal euphemism, 'forfeit of the law'; Isabella kicks it upstairs, makes 'forfeit' resonate in its universal, theological sense: she makes Claudio's case heard in a court where Christ is judge. Rhythmically, the speech gives a clue that she's beginning to take off. The pulse becomes more regular, and all those firm masculine endings to the lines seem to take her from strength to strength. But then the speech resolves into such generous, open sensuousness: the 'o' sounds, and 'mmm', 'nnn', 'thhh', 'www', and open vowels that could go on for ever. She's sensually connecting with the argument. It's no longer the pounding rhythms of the first lines. The last two lines are expansive, liberal, as generous as the 'mercy' she is extolling.

Even then she doesn't win. Angelo says, 'He dies tomorrow.' That 'tomorrow' knocks Isabella sideways. As always, the punctuation is a breathing clue, and the breath tells you what the thought is doing. Isabella is almost winded. She keeps gulping air: 'Tomorrow? [breath] O, [breath] that's sudden; [breath] spare him, [breath] spare him [breath].' Shakespeare gives you five pauses that you must take, to physicalise her shock. Then each phrase gets slightly longer. She's punched, but she doesn't go under. Like many female characters in Shakespeare, she's not rendered inarticulate by emotional shock. The blood goes from her gut to her head. She deals with it, and it releases her into a new area of argument.

That's what Paola meant when she observed that Juliet was 'married to the text, and the text fed her into higher and higher energy levels'. This Isabella was never flattened because the pulse that kept her lines moving kept the character moving too. Juliet comments:

The importance of working on a text in this rigorous way – line by line, image by image, breath by breath – is that you discover what a speech is actually about instead of what you assumed it was about. In Shakespeare you must always play what's there, not what you think is there. This working method imposed a strict discipline that I found illuminating when I got to the soliloquy in II, iv, which I've described as the trickiest moment of the play for the actress playing Isabella. What I learned is that 'More than our brother is our chastity' is neither the premise of the speech nor its conclusion. The soliloquy starts somewhere else and finishes somewhere else. And what happens first in the speech teaches you how to speak the difficult line. And it also, I think, tells you that the speech is not about chastity, it's about anarchy.

> To whom should I complain? Did I tell this,
> Who would believe me? O perilous mouths,
> That bear in them one and the selfsame tongue,
> Either of condemnation or approof,
> Bidding the law make curtsy to their will,
> Hooking both right and wrong to th'appetite,
> To follow as it draws.

These lines became central to my interpretation. I discovered in them an Isabella who is confronting the collapse of values, of beliefs, of justice, of virtue. If condemnation and approof speak with the same tongue, if the same 'perilous mouth' that is condemning her brother for fornication is soliciting her, and if there is no appeal to justice because the judge himself is corrupt, that's chaos; by saying 'yes' to Angelo, Isabella would be committing herself to chaos. It's not her chastity that's at stake, it's order. Insisting on her virtue isn't a priggish affectation she defends at the cost of her brother's life. It's the last redoubt holding out against the chaos that threatens to overrun it. Dangerously, the very rhythms of the speech propel Isabella towards a feeling of 'you *could* give in!' The acceleration, the growing exhilaration, push her towards giving in. The line 'More than our brother' puts the brakes on. It is more than a personal decision: it has political resonances too.

How did Isabella's play end for Juliet?

Our director wanted it to end as comedy – he meant comedy as defined by a resolved ending. But we discovered that a resolved ending really depends on the Duke. He's the one who has set in motion everything that has happened in *Measure for Measure*; he's the one who has manipulated the whole sequence of events, and most of the characters. The last act is a trial that exposes everyone but also gives them a chance to redeem themselves. The last character to be put on trial is the Duke. Having meted out all those judgements, he turns round, and there's Lucio! Lucio, who's slandered him, abused him, dogged him with calumny. And the Duke says, 'Hang him!'

As Isabella, I stood and looked at him. Watched to see what he would do. Because unless the Duke takes on the trial of *himself*, which involves bringing himself to let Lucio off the hook, to exercise forgiveness, he hasn't learned the capacity for mercy from Isabella, and there is no justification for a 'happy' ending. Nothing mutual has been established between them. He watched me watching, turned back to Lucio, and reprieved the death sentence.

But you know, there isn't a fixed end to a play. The *script* ends. The words run out. But the *ending* – that's something that has to be renegotiated every performance.

Shakespeare gives Isabella no words at the end. Maybe because she doesn't know what to say to the Duke's proposal, 'Give me thy hand.' It's often the case with the female protagonists: discounting the Epilogue, Rosalind doesn't speak for the last twenty minutes of *As You Like It*. The status quo has been restored. Men are organising things. So what should Isabella say or do? I used to take a long, long pause, in which I looked at everyone – drawing in the collective experience in a way. Then I took the Duke's hand.

Oh, just for the record. The reviewers got it wrong. Paola's Isabella was wonderful. I know. I was there every night.

3
Lady Macbeth's Barren Sceptre

Sinead Cusack graduated to Lady Macbeth from an apprenticeship in RSC takeovers – moving into parts created by other actresses – and a confident coming-of-age in a succession of major roles: Celia, Portia, Kate, Beatrice. She doesn't hold with glorifying her profession: in her terms, acting is not a mystery but a craft, and her roles emerge very practically out of the stuff of daily life. When she talks about her working methods, she moves rapidly from general observation to specific roles.

I am not an analytical actress. I work off gut intuition and what I'm getting from other actors on stage. I think I'm quite strong in rehearsals. I'm known to hold my views.

I did something I'd never done before when I took over Isabella in *Measure for Measure* [1979]. I learnt my lines before I went in on the first day of rehearsal. We had a very short rehearsal period – I'd taken over the part from Paola Dionisotti for the London run – and I was in a panic; the only thing I could concentrate on was getting a handle on Isabella and trying to understand her, the positions she took, the journey she made.

I got into her through my own Irish Catholic convent upbringing. I remember when we used to have retreats and everyone would get very holy. I got pretty holy myself and promised all sorts of things, like making bargains with God about chastity. It all went by the wayside when I got a bit older, but it helped me understand the value system that Isabella feels she has to adhere to. I enjoyed the journey of that play. I enjoyed trying to understand her own narrowness of vision – which is not to do with not sleeping with Angelo, that's not an area that I found narrow in her, I found that right. What I found narrow was that she was judgemental. She was judgemental about everyone at the beginning of the play, but at the end, she no longer was. She somehow has been given a humanity and a wisdom.

Sinead is characteristically more inclined to see where she 'failed' in a role rather than where she wonderfully succeeded. And she did not start out professionally with a reservoir of confidence.

Shakespeare used to frighten the wits out of me because I was too reverent about it; I didn't smile because I thought that would be wrong. I approached each speech as a 'speech', and I looked at the syntax and the verbal shapes, and as a result I was one of the most boring Shakespearean actors in the world.

And then I had a Saul on the road to Damascus number in the BBC TV production of *Twelfth Night*. I was playing Olivia, doing a scene with Viola, and I began to *talk*, and I suddenly thought, 'She's real, this person is real', and I started to smile and cough and scratch my ear and do normal things. Since then I've never dared approach a text in the analytical way I used to, in case I slip back. Now I only look for a woman.

Another transforming experience in her personal life was the birth of her first son.

When he was born he completely changed my perspective on the theatre and acting. He gave me courage, which I'd never had before – I used to be intimidated by the process of acting, it scared me, and as a result I was very bad in many roles. He gave me courage because he put the business of acting where it should be, made it something that you do for a living. If you're lucky, you touch the heart of the audience or give them a little vision.

Early in the 1986 Stratford season, Sinead Cusack told the director of *Macbeth*, Adrian Noble, that some elements in the role of Lady Macbeth would be problematic for her.

He said, 'What do you mean?' and I said, 'I've just given birth! I have another baby. I'm going to find that area of her very difficult . . .' He told me not to worry, but I was very worried, because every time I came to that line 'I have given suck, and know/How tender 'tis . . .' – I can't say it even now – I thought, 'I'm never going to be able to speak that line. Not while I'm nursing my own baby.' You're always left a bit raw after having a baby; I felt very vulnerable, and I was worried about that element coming into play too much in Lady Macbeth, but in fact I was able to incorporate that rawness into my own performance.

Indeed, the idea of maternity came close to the centre of her performance and the whole production. Sinead had strong images of Lady Macbeth and her relationship with Macbeth.

I wanted people to see someone who had warmth and fecundity; I liked the idea of her hair being fair. I didn't see her as a very clever woman – she is a grasper of opportunity.

She knows she has Macbeth in thrall and she can make him do anything. And yet she has no knowledge of the hell that she's letting loose in his mind and his life, and what he will become. Never for a second does she have a notion of that.

In fact, she had begun imagining her Lady Macbeth when she was still a teenager:

from about the age of fifteen, when I first read the play. I wanted to play her very young because I had a sense of a Lady Macbeth I had never seen. I wanted her to be young, very beautiful, and to have a sort of amorality, a complete ignorance of right and wrong, the sort of blinkered vision of a child who grabs what it wants with no thought of the consequence. I wanted a woman in white. That vision lived with me throughout my twenties, but no one asked me to play it. I hadn't the craft or the skills, and anyway no one had that view of the role. It was traditionally played by someone older. In black.

It wasn't until she was in her late thirties – ironically, too old to qualify for the part in her fantasy, but now mature enough in her craft to attempt it – that she was offered Lady Macbeth opposite Jonathan Pryce. The character she had outlined in her head, however, still survived virtually intact.

I told Adrian about this vision of mine and we thought how we might bring an element of it to bear. One of the things I was adamant about right from the beginning was that the first view you would have of the Macbeths would be of a successful, blessed couple. I wanted the audience to be drawn to them right from the beginning of the play. Macbeth – a poet, warrior, philosopher, an extraordinary man of vision, adored by everyone around him. They all speak of him in hushed tones. Married to this beautiful woman. Macbeth and his wife are the golden couple – like the Kennedys – who have everything.

Everything, that is, except one thing: they have no children.

Lady Macbeth says, 'I have given suck . . .' So where is that baby?
What happened to their child? I'm not certain who asked the
question first or whether we all had the idea simultaneously, but as
we explored it in rehearsal, we decided that the Macbeths had had a
child and that the child had died. The line can be interpreted
differently, but that's the interpretation we chose, and as the idea
grew it seemed to have a beautiful logic.

So as rehearsals progressed, it was this bleak biological datum – 'He
hath no children' – that began to focus the tragedy. *Macbeth* became
not so much a political tragedy of multiple betrayal as a domestic
drama, the destruction of a marriage. Lacking children, the Macbeths'
energies redirected themselves into obsessions that travestied
creativity: they killed other people's children, turning their kingdom
into a wasteland. But when they discovered what it meant to hold a
barren sceptre, their childlessness doubly mocked them. There could
be no success without succession.

The image of the lost child became the most potent reference point
in Noble's production. First suggested in a blood-smeared child
rescued from the battlefield in the opening scene, it reappeared in
other bloody children: the one who rises from the witches' cauldron,
the one who 'from my mother's womb untimely ripped' – Macduff –
bleeds Macbeth at the end.

This Macbeth liked having children around. He liked children's
games. The witches' apparitions were children, seductive in white
nightgowns, playing blind man's buff with the kneeling king on the floor,
giggling their predictions into his ear, then circling him in an endless
procession of Banquo's future issue. These same white-gowned
children then became Macduff's ambushed family. One of them sat on
the floor playing with the assassin's bootstraps before he was picked
up and stabbed.

Sinead felt that such images found a contemporary expression for
the evil that the play is exploring. The abuse of children is the ultimate
taboo, the death of a child the ultimate grief.

That sort of loss, the loss of a child, is so huge, so massive, that it can
either draw you closer together or separate you, or it can turn the
need for a child into an obsessive need for something else. If you've
lost a child and there are no more children, you either leave the man
or you become obsessive about the man and about his happiness and

security. That's the avenue I chose to go up as Lady Macbeth – that she had turned, not in on herself, but completely in on him.

Marital claustrophobia became a key image of the production as a whole.

But Adrian and I didn't really talk about the play until the eve of the first rehearsal. That wasn't a good idea. I kept asking to be involved in discussions; Jonathan Pryce was allowed to participate but not me. I wanted to talk to the designer, Bob Crowley – but that didn't happen either. Eventually we had a meeting in London and I was shown the set model and costume designs.

There it was – my nightmare! I was dressed in black, the set was a black box. Macbeth was in black. I thought, 'This is it, this is the production I didn't want to be in.' They said, 'What do you want?' and I said, 'I want to be in white, or anything but black. Don't predispose the audience right from the beginning of the play to the tragedy and horror and evil. That'll come. But *let* it come.'

Sinead won on the dress. She played Lady Macbeth in green. ('They wouldn't countenance white.') She first appeared not as the black widow spider of theatre tradition but as a slight green figure with a broad halo of fair hair.

She changed her mind about the black box. She came to see it as 'an inspired piece of design' that 'helped us as actors because it had a wonderful theatrical sense'. It began as a battlefield, impaled with a thicket of torn battle standards, across which three shuffling hags picked their way, rolling over corpses, salvaging from under one that live but blood-soaked child. When, at the end of the battle sequence, these flags were struck by Duncan's victorious army, the black box became Dunsinane, an emptied-out space that seemed vast because it contained only the small figure of Lady Macbeth. For Sinead, the place seemed double.

That first entrance, when I walked on stage and I had those black walls around me, I could feel I was actually on the battlements of the castle – I had a very strong sense of that, I always brought it on with me – but at the same time I could have been in one of those small stone rooms that are found in Scottish castles.

Bob Crowley's set often had this paradoxical sense of seeming to double as something else. It was an illusionist's box where any number of conjuror's tricks might defeat the eye. Doors suddenly appeared, stairs shot out of flush walls. Then the walls themselves began to move. The Macbeths' world got smaller and smaller until it felt like a coffin.

Pryce played Macbeth as a man who lurched from hero to madman to clown, first armour-plated and draped in black tartan, then bizarrely clerical, finally clownish, ending up in huge boots and slack stockings. He rolled up his shirt-sleeves before killing Duncan.

Sinead's Lady Macbeth marked her journey to confusion with equivalent landmarks: sensual, intimate with her husband before the murder; rigid behind a cosmetic mask after the coronation; transformed into a demented child in the sleepwalking scene. Her first entrance (I, v) was restless, almost fugitive. She was clutching a letter, the one in which Macbeth reports the witches' prediction. She was looking for somewhere to read it alone.

The decision you have to make about the letter is whether she's read it before, whether it's a letter she's had clasped to her bosom for some time. After trying out various things, I came to the conclusion that she had just been handed the letter, and that she'd headed for that particular space in order to read it. It was interesting how we arrived at that isolation. There are other choices, you know. It doesn't have to be as isolated as we made it, and it certainly doesn't have to be as still as we made it.

During rehearsal I was experimenting all over the place. I couldn't say the lines without moving. I was using my hands, my body, I was all over the stage. At one point I sat in front of a mirror and daubed lipstick all over my face, but I still found I couldn't simply say the lines: I hadn't got the courage. And then finally one day Adrian said, 'Just cut out all of that, just stand in the middle of the stage and say them,' and I found it very difficult indeed.

In Sinead's performance the words of the letter tumbled out. Her eyes could scarcely keep pace with her mouth, which seemed already to know what the letter contained:

> 'They met me in the day of success, and I have learned by the perfectest report they have more in them than mortal knowledge. When I burned in desire to question them further, they made themselves air, into which they vanished . . . these Weird Sisters saluted me, and referred me to the coming on of time with, "Hail, king that shalt be." '

When she reads that letter it's almost uncanny for her, because she thinks, 'This supernatural news that he's giving me about these three sisters is confirming something that I had already envisioned, that we had already talked about.' The letter is almost familiar to her. That experience with the Weird Sisters – almost as if she knew it would happen. It's as if suddenly everything comes right. Macbeth *ought* to be Duncan's successor. There was no blood succession in Scotland, the crown was not handed on to the son automatically. Macbeth was the *natural* heir. They had talked about his succession.

Had they discussed the murder of Duncan? I don't think they had. But they had talked about Macbeth being King.

Her own view, the one she'd always held, was that if he wasn't named successor by Duncan then the way through would be to kill. Suddenly, there's the letter with its supernatural news – and the whole universe is endorsing her view, saying to her, 'You're right, your vision is correct, and here's the proof.' The idea is familiar because she's been through it all in her head already. And here it is: 'You're on the right track. You have every right to this. He deserves it.'

Macbeth is a capable killer. His reported soldiership in scene ii proves that. But can he murder?

She knows that where he's weak is in the honour stakes. He's got too much honour. So he's a little bit susceptible, his honour might take away his courage at the crucial moment of murder.

Lady Macbeth was strong enough for both. In the first half of her first soliloquy she weighed up her husband, tapping the folded letter against her palm:

> Glamis thou art, and Cawdor, and shalt be
> What thou art promised. Yet do I fear thy nature:
>   . . .What thou wouldst highly
> That wouldst thou holily, wouldst not play false,
> And yet wouldst wrongly win.

Lady Macbeth's naïve assessment of her husband's nature constantly stunned Sinead when she detached herself from the role and looked at the character.

She has this extraordinary seeming knowledge of him, that he may not be able to do it: *if she did but know*! And it's only seeming knowledge because Lady Macbeth has no real knowledge of what he will become. She lacks imagination.

She was musing in the soliloquy, musing about him. The actual acceptance of killing, and the acceptance of Duncan being killed, had already taken place in her mind. But murder – that sort of killing was against everything Macbeth believes in. He is an 'honourable man'. She's on to him so fast: how will *I* persuade him? How will *I* deal with it? How will *I* kill . . . It seemed to me at this point in this scene that the murderer is going to be her. She will kill.

And then it happens again. Another of those supernatural markers drops her way, as if confirming her route. A messenger enters. 'The King comes here tonight.' She can't believe her ears. 'Thou'rt mad to say it!' Sinead's Lady Macbeth was instantly alert.

The minute she sees the opening she says, '*Now* we do it. Now's the perfect time – everything is right. Duncan is being given to us on a plate.'

But then a new misgiving shook her. Would *she* be strong enough? Lady Macbeth dismissed the messenger. Vulnerable and alone, she began to pray:

> Come, you spirits
> That tend on mortal thoughts, unsex me here
> And fill me from the crown to the toe top-full
> Of direst cruelty . . . Come to my woman's breasts
> And take my milk for gall, you murdering ministers.

Sinead saw the speech as a bargain struck with those 'murdering ministers': she was willing to renounce her sexuality, her erotic power over Macbeth, in exchange for that other power, the kind that comes with a crown.

In rehearsal one of the areas we explored was their sexual obsession. Sexually he was totally dependent on her. He *needed* that sex in order to reassure himself of his own values, his own strength. And she knows, she knows she can play on that. She knows she can get him to do things because of that. And she uses it.

In the soliloquy she is saying, 'I will throw away my sexuality, I will give it up, I will never enjoy those areas again, I will never have children again – if I can have this. It's a bargain I've made with the devil. In order to achieve this for him, I will deny my *self*.'

Yet the pernicious bargain was more, it was an admission of vulnerability.

Lady Macbeth knows that she loves Macbeth. She knows that she has tenderness and vulnerability where he is concerned. She knows that that is her weakness, that she is capable of love. Love of a child, love of a man. So now, when all the signs are saying, 'The time is right,' and pointing her the way she must urge him to go, she says, 'I can't do it. I've got to get help from outside. I can't do it on my own because my love will let me be weakened into letting him fail.' She invokes the spirits to make her strong. Not 'unsex me' – make me an un-woman, a pseudo-man; but 'unsex me' – make me invulnerable to love. And then Macbeth walks on stage and she plays the old games.

Pryce's Macbeth materialised behind her, out of a black hole at the back.

I didn't see him; I felt him. What we wanted was for him to be completely silent but for her to know that he's there by a kind of kinetic energy they both react to. (How did I know he was there? That isn't mysterious – Jonathan pants on stage.)

The effect was of two white faces eerily superimposed on one another while their bodies, miles apart, recoiled as if from a physical shock. That physical energy became transferred to the words, all those interweaving half-lines.

We became locked into each other's language:

> *Macbeth*   My dearest love,
>   Duncan comes here tonight.
> *Lady Macbeth*   And when goes hence?
>   *Macbeth* Tomorrow, as he purposes.
> *Lady Macbeth*   O never
>   Shall sun that morrow see!

We felt that there was a kind of synchronicity between them. It's as if they're in tune with each other's minds. They're so enmeshed, the couple. When they grow apart, at the end of the murder scene, you find that they're talking different languages, but here they both

know what they are talking about. So we didn't kiss on the greeting –
'My dearest love' – we decided to face the business first. After
'Never/Shall sun that morrow see!' it's as if the kiss is a
confirmation of both their thoughts, a physical sealing of a compact.
The way Jonathan played it, it's as if Macbeth *needed* to be enclosed
by her, in order to be able to deal with the idea, to encompass it. He
clung to me like the lines cling to each other.

And then Lady Macbeth says, 'He that's coming/Must be
provided for.' It's an amazing line. She's going to play hostess to
Duncan at Dunsinane, and 'provide' is what gracious hostesses
always do. It's a wonder of a line to play because the reverberations
do the acting for you, make the audience go 'Aaaagh!'

'Provided for' here means murdered, and the poise of her euphemism
marks her detachment. Not from her husband – they left the scene 'hanging on to each other' – but from the killing. 'You notice she never actually says, "kill".' The Macbeths would never be closer than in that exit.
In the following scene (I, vi) they were already unaccountably apart.
Duncan arrives at Dunsinane, but Macbeth is not at the door to greet
him. For Lady Macbeth, playing hostess,

that was very awkward . . . Both should have been there. But he's
not. She apologises, and Duncan makes a joke of it, but it is a
departure from protocol that is noted. She's covering up for him.
She knows he can't face that ceremony because of what he is about
to do. So she substitutes for him, with great eloquence and ritual.
And we never see Macbeth with Duncan again.

Sinead considers the direction of this scene 'inspired'. Duncan's battle-
weary men, still grimy with blood and dirt, were slumped against the
castle walls, waiting.

All those rough soldiers were lying around, and then this woman
swept through them in a green dress and a red shawl. To those men
she was like a vision, a drink of water in the desert. I felt very
strongly that the scene had to be beautiful, and she had to look
welcoming, to highlight the horror of what she was doing – and all
those men had to react to her, either sexually or as if to a mother,
but all of them had to react.

They did. Men who looked dead came alive, and followed her into
Dunsinane.

Sinead's view of Lady Macbeth as society hostess came to the fore in the following scene (I, vii), when her husband failed her yet again. Dinner was being served somewhere off stage. *Again* Macbeth had departed from protocol.

Very, very badly. We're supposed to be entertaining the King at a banquet in his honour, and Macbeth left Duncan, he left the King, and to cap it all, he didn't come back! Imagine – he gets up and leaves and people think, oh, it's a phone call or he's gone to have a pee, but fifteen, twenty minutes elapse, and the King is sitting there . . . That's frivolous, but if you put it in a modern context – the Kennedys again – you can see how much it mattered.

In fact, Macbeth had fled, seeking refuge where he could hammer things out: 'If it were done when 'tis done, then 'twere well / It were done quickly.' But what if it's not done when it's done; what if that is only the beginning?

Lady Macbeth pursued him. This time it was she who materialised out of the doorway behind, blocking all the light that had flooded through it from the banqueting hall, condensing it into a grotesque shadow. Her question 'Why have you left the chamber?' was not looking for an answer but for a fight.

She has to get him. She knows she has to strengthen his resolve. So she goads him as far as she can, sexually and in all kinds of ways. 'Was the hope drunk?' 'Art thou afeard?' *Are you a man?* Is this all you're worth? She uses everything! Every weapon.

But as I was saying the words, part of me was also silently appealing to him, soothing him, as if he were a child: 'I know what you're going through, and I don't want you to be going through it.' But she herself found the strength from somewhere (maybe those 'murdering ministers' stepped in!) not to take him in her arms and say, 'Hush, hush, it's all right, you needn't do it.'

Because he *has* to do it; there is a higher purpose. Macbeth covered his head with his arms to block out the relentless noise, then lashed out: he slapped her hard across the mouth. It stunned her, but she continued her verbal battering:

She goes on and on and on, and finally when she sees that her clever tongue, her sexuality, her goading, nothing is going to work on him

– then she pulls out the one area that she's never used, the secret area of the child . . .

The slap – for the Macbeths that moment was nothing. That slap was part of our natural physicality. Jonathan did hit me every night, and made the unfortunate mistake of saying so in the press, and someone wrote in saying, 'Why is she such a wimp to take it?' But the scene was such that I believe if we'd done a fake slap, we would have destroyed that electric current of violence between us. I shouldn't admit these things because actors should be able to fake slaps very easily and still be able to keep the mood, but I was convinced we wouldn't be able to sustain that extraordinary power if we were doing a fake number. I much preferred a stinging slap every night. Technically Jonathan is very clever and I think only on three occasions did he get me on the jawbone, but mostly it was absolutely flat on and it would sting for a minute and then it was gone.

The slap was a step in a process of escalation. But it was not the critical moment. The critical moment was what came next, the area she'd never used, the secret area of the child. 'I have given suck, and know/How tender 'tis to love the babe that milks me.' But she would have 'dashed the brains out, had I so sworn as you/Have done to this'. What she says about the baby, and his reaction to it, is completely divorced from their natural exchange. The use of the baby – that was the worst, that was the real sin. And that's when he knows how much she wants this for him, when he understands the sacrifice that she's making. And that's when he grabbed her, held her, and they were both crying.

His response to his barren wife was a bit of a joke: 'Bring forth men-children only!' He was trying to regain control. He was using black humour to restore things to some kind of equilibrium.

Pryce's Macbeth constantly faced crisis with clowning. Later, the role would trap him, but for now, he saw the immediate future, the murder, as a huge joke. What a joke it would be to smear Duncan's servants with his blood! They left the scene laughing, but sharing the joke meant sharing the job.

And while Macbeth was about it, Lady Macbeth was alone again on stage.

She is very frightened. She says, 'The doors are open.' She sees what he is doing, not actually, but in her mind; she is imagining it as it happened and she's beginning to fracture. The line, 'Had he not resembled/My father as he slept, I had done't,' shocks her. She's trying to hang on. And then she hears a noise, and she goes to the stairs, and then he erupts from the chamber. Panic, panic, panic! She doesn't understand what he's talking about – the language is coming apart! She says to him,

Lady Macbeth Did you not speak?
      Macbeth   When?
Lady Macbeth   Now.
      Macbeth   As I descended?
Lady Macbeth Ay.
      Macbeth Hark.

And then she sees the blood. Now in that moment when she sees the blood, something happens to her gut. For her, the sight is horrible. It shocks her, the reality of it. She has imagined the killing, but people who have visions are often shocked by the reality when it comes. When she faces the blood on his hands it's like a blow to the stomach. And then she gets over it. As an actress I tried to show just a little click in my brain that I could store up to use and refer back to later when I had blood on my own hands.

After that we began talking different languages. We who had needed to touch each other all the time grew distant. When he had killed, neither of us wanted to touch the other.

She tried to follow him, tried to understand.

She's saying, 'What do you mean, you heard voices?' She's trying to make it practical: well, of course, 'There are two lodged together,' that's why you heard the voices saying a prayer. And he says, 'I could not say "amen",' and she says, 'Consider it not so deeply': it doesn't matter. But she realises he's gone somewhere that she doesn't understand; she can't bring him back. It's as if she's seeing him drifting, drifting, she's trying to pull him back, but he won't come.

Because she's been frightened by seeing the blood, she can't bring her usual power to bear. I wanted to touch him, but he drew away. We couldn't do what we were used to doing. For the first time in our lives. We weren't touching. And she's panicking.

Then she sees that he's brought the daggers! God – he was so stupid! I shrieked at him. That was the Irish fishwife in me. But he wouldn't take them back. So I did. Trying to make it practical. She went up those stairs – she rubbed her hands in Duncan's blood – and the woman who came down those stairs was a child. She was stretching out her hands like a child – half guilty, half defiant.

The fingers were splayed, the shoulders slightly hunched, the eyes feverish, the intonation a child's.

Something's clicked in her brain. Again, she's taken too much. It was a character shift. I don't know where it came from – stretching out the hands like a child – but it was a great help to me for her descent into the murky areas below.

This gesture, which Sinead would repeat in the sleepwalking scene in Act IV, marked the crossroads. From now on, Lady Macbeth was different: the wife of the murderer became Queen of Scotland. And as Queen, Sinead did wear black.

The next time we see her she has been crowned and she is dressed in full regalia, in a black velvet dress, tightly corseted, a Tudor cape up to her ears, a ruff that came right up to her chin, and the crown on top. When I had to put on those huge heavy robes I thought I'd never be able to bear the weight – it was amazing to stand there bowed down by those clothes. It was a great design point. It's a play that's constantly talking about borrowed robes.

I was very keen that the softness we had seen in her first scene – the hair, the warm make-up, the ruffles down her back – should be gone. After the coronation I wanted her to be very constricted – her hair pulled back, her skin almost stretched across her cheek-bones, whitened, and with blood-red lipstick on – I hadn't worn lipstick before. It was a cover-up, saying, 'Now I am the Queen, and I will look like the Queen,' while at the same time she was disintegrating inside. From that point onwards she is keeping the façade up – and the façade is magnificent.

There was more killing to be done but Lady Macbeth had no stomach for it.

In rehearsal we discussed endlessly whether she knew Macbeth was going to kill Banquo, and we came to the conclusion that indeed she did, and she didn't want him to do it. She had switched strategies entirely. Her view was, 'Look, we've got it. You're King! It doesn't *matter* whether they suspect, you're inviolate. We cannot be touched!' But she knows he's contemplating the next one, and she thinks,

'No, no, it's getting out of hand, don't take that further step . . .'

Macbeth and Lady Macbeth have a little scene (III, ii) just after he has organised Banquo's murder. She starts the scene with a servant, asking him to tell the King she'd like to speak with him. And then, alone, she says, 'Naught's had, all's spent,/Where our desire is got without content.' It's so poignant and so bewildered. She's saying, 'I've got everything I wanted for him, and he's got everything he ever wanted, but we have no contentment. *Why?*' She doesn't understand. She hasn't faced any of the realities – there's just this blind, blinkered vision of what life is going to be.

'How now, my Lord? Why do you keep alone,' her line to Macbeth when he entered, was very plaintive; it meant, 'Why don't you love me any more?' She knows that not only has she lost his love, she has lost her power as well, power to change him or to comfort him. Without him loving her, she can't do anything for him. Or with him. She knows it – he's drifting, drifting, and she can't follow.

And he's frightening her now, too. He's talking of more killing. He says, 'Thou know'st that Banquo and his Fleance live.' That's when she knows he's going to kill again, and that he's going to kill Fleance, he's going to *kill the child.*

They had completely reversed roles now. Lady Macbeth needed no more. She didn't care about what was out there, she had what she wanted – for him. But he needs to secure his position now, and keep his paranoia at bay by killing off anyone who's suspicious. And she knows he's going to kill the child! It's excruciating . . .

But then, just for a moment, it looked as if everything was going to be all right. He came very close to me – 'Come, seeling night,/Scarf up the tender eye of pitiful day' – and he passed his hand across my face, and we were about to kiss, and she thought, 'It's going to be all right! Thank God! He wants to kiss me!'

And we're getting closer, and it's going to be all right, and then the maniac reared his head. He suddenly shouted, 'Waaaaww!' and I jumped. It was horrible, horrible. And then he smeared all my lipstick across my face. He put his hand in my mouth and yanked down my jaw, mocking a kiss. It was a travesty of the embrace, of how it used to be. He was throwing their sexuality back in her face, saying, 'That no longer has power in my life,' scoffing at her with that bark of a laugh. His mania was staggeringly dangerous and she was terrified, terrified. And deeply hurt. Lost.

By the end of the banquet, two scenes later, Lady Macbeth knew that

the marriage was over. The scene (III, iv) was set on a narrow strip
along the front of the stage, across its entire width.

A bit of the stage rose up; a white sheet covered it: that was our
'table'. Macbeth was at one end and Lady Macbeth was at the other
and all the Thanes were sitting with their backs to the audience. We
did the gracious bit – 'Everybody have a nice time' – and then
Macbeth went berserk! He suddenly shouted, 'Which of you have
done this?' Nobody knew what he was talking about.
    And then we were having this terrible row, the King and Queen,
right in the middle of the Thanes. Normally directors set the
argument to the side.
    The embarrassment of all those people watching . . . awful! She
was trying to cut the others out, trying to stop him and he was going
on and on, he just didn't see them, didn't care about them. It was the
most embarrassing thing you could imagine for a wife. She was
saying through clenched teeth, 'Don't do this here, *please*, let's get
out,' trying to ease him out, 'let's do it somewhere else, just don't do
it in front of them!'
    Because the Thanes' backs were to the audience, everything was
cast on our two faces. I could sense them, their embarrassment, their
suspicion, watching to see him incriminate himself.

Lady Macbeth saw her husband on the brink of madness and, despite
her façade, knew that she was there too. Unlike him, though, she didn't
see Banquo's ghost.

It was terribly dangerous, because I didn't know what he was
talking about!
    At the end of the banquet scene I remember sitting watching him
across that table – we couldn't have been farther apart, and there's
such a lot of time for Lady Macbeth to watch him in the scene –
watching, and knowing that in my attempt to give him what I
believed he wanted, I had unleashed a monster. He was completely
gone from me and he would never come back. It was a feeling of
absolute hopelessness. It was complete loss.

In one of his convulsive gestures, lunging at a spectre no one else could
see, Macbeth had pulled the table-cloth off the table. Then he sat stiffly,
his Thanes having scattered in disarray, trying to repair the damage by
smoothing out the table-cloth.

Above
Macbeth 1986
Sinead Cusack, Lady Macbeth
Jonathan Pryce, Macbeth
The married couple agreed on murder I, vii

Left
Macbeth 1986
Sinead Cusack, Lady Macbeth
Reading Macbeth's letter I, v

Far left
Macbeth 1986
Sinead Cusack, Lady Macbeth
The sleepwalking scene V, i

Left
All's Well That Ends Well 1981
Harriet Walter, Helena
Dame Peggy Ashcroft, the Countess
Women in mourning
at Rossillion I, i

Below
All's Well That Ends Well 1981
Harriet Walter, Helena
John Franklyn-Robbins, King of France
Persuading the King to live II, i

Left
All's Well That Ends Well 1981
Harriet Walter, Helena
Mike Gwilym, Bertram
John Franklyn-Robbins, King
The King gives Bertram to Helena II, iii

Below
Cymbeline 1987
Harriet Walter, Imogen
David Bradley, Cymbeline
Nicholas Farrell, Posthumus
Reuniting the Kingdom
in a 'gracious season' V, v

Below
Cymbeline 1987
Harriet Walter, Imogen
Imogen asks news of her banished husband   I, iii

Above
As You Like It 1985
Juliet Stevenson, Rosalind
Fiona Shaw, Celia
Plotting elopement to Arden I, iii

Right
As You Like It 1985
Fiona Shaw, Celia
Urging Rosalind, 'Be merry!' I, ii

Above
As You Like It 1985
Juliet Stevenson, Rosalind/Ganymede
Disguised for wooing games in Arden III, ii

Above
As You Like It 1985
Juliet Stevenson, Rosalind
Fiona Shaw, Celia
Hilton MacRae, Orlando
Mock wedding in Arden IV, i

Left
As You Like It 1985
Juliet Stevenson, Rosalind
Fiona Shaw, Celia
Refugees in Arden II, iv

It was so banal, that gesture of setting the table again! That's what I liked about our production. Again and again we were allowed as actors to not be those huge tragic figures but sometimes to be terribly domestic, terribly mundane, so that it brought the level of that evil into an area we all know.

The Macbeths were once again alone. Physically, though, they were estranged, polarised at opposite ends of the table. Macbeth had been changed by killing and he no longer needed her.

She's been replaced by this sort of mania, this paranoia. She says at the end of the scene, 'You lack the season of all natures, sleep.' I put my hand through his hair. It was the first time he'd let me touch him since the murder, and he took my hand and he held it to his face in *agony*. Then he just dropped it: 'Come, we'll to sleep.' As if he'd said, 'Right,' like clapping up a bargain on some livestock, 'let's go to bed.' The way Jonathan played that line was wonderful! So threatening. That's when she realised the full extent of his madness.

And she recoiled from the word 'sleep' because it wasn't a natural continuation of the touch. In the normal run of things, if we'd touched in that way we would indeed have gone to bed. But the way he said it I knew we wouldn't be going to bed to love each other, there wouldn't be a natural continuation of any gentleness: that would never happen again. What he went on to say was even worse: 'My strange and self-abuse/Is the initiate fear that wants hard use.' That is, 'I need more, I've got to have more, *I want more killing.*' 'We are yet but young in deed' wasn't weary or desperate. It was apologetic. He meant, 'Look, I'm sorry about what happened at the banquet. I was feeling a bit shaky, and the reason I fell apart was that, actually, I haven't had enough practice, that's all. I'll get better.' But he'd left her behind. He'd gone. Literally. He walked off stage.

Lady Macbeth followed behind. The witches – the director shifted a scene here – were coming on, picking up bits of the ruined banquet to use for their cauldron scene. She saw them. She looked at them, and then she looked away as if to say, 'No, I'm not seeing that,' and exited. There was no shock or recoil. It was just the meshing of two worlds.

Or the unhinging of a mind. The separate exits marked their divorce, took them into different worlds. Macbeth sought out other women – he went to the witches – while Lady Macbeth went mad. And although the play itself broadens out, as the scene shifts to England and follows Malcolm's march on Scotland, Macbeth's walls were closing in and Lady Macbeth's world had shrunk to a single room where she walked in her sleep and played out, night after night, the murder of Duncan.

For the actress, there is now a long off-stage wait, until V, i.

I would go to my dressing room and have a great time – a strong cup of tea, a fag – and then I messed myself up. People hated the way I looked in the sleepwalking scene and I don't give a tuppenny! I loved it.

I had on this gown of white cotton, almost like a hospital gown, and then I had Macbeth's jumper on – the one he'd worn under his armour: she'd been sleeping in it. I wanted to give the impression that she'd been in that nightgown for a long time, that she wasn't dressing during the day, and the nightgown was soiled. And then one day in rehearsal – it's ridiculous how these things happen, they have no logic to them – Adrian said to me, 'Tuck the nightie up into your knickers, I think you're going to paddle in the sea.' Of course – washing her hands!

I'm a sleepwalker myself. Once when I was a child my parents were having a party; at about eleven o'clock I emerged from my bedroom and I walked through the hallway into the garden and took off my nightie. I dug a hole in the garden and I buried my nightdress. And then I went back to bed. My parents told me that my sleepwalking was characterised by speed. I was very *busy* in my sleep, and I found that a great help, coming down fast, in the sleepwalking scene. I felt that her particular brand of unrest would be those frantic little devil-thoughts that you can't knock out of your mind, devil-thoughts that keep coming back – about blood, about *blood*. You know when you're panicking, frantically panicking, and these little shooting thoughts are hitting you and getting embroiled and all mixed up in your head and you can't stop the voices, you can't stop the sounds: that's the sort of unrest I pictured her as having, and that's certainly the way the sleepwalking speech is written – erratic, disjointed.

What I found I had to do in rehearsal was to clarify absolutely in my head what each of those thoughts reminded me of, what situations they were pictures of. It's terribly easy to generalise madness or unrest or panic into one long blur, but you have to isolate each single thought so that it's absolutely clear to you where the picture – where those words – comes from. It took me ages and ages to do that.

I ran down the stairs and then I turned and I held out my hands – it was that same spasmodic child gesture from after the murder when I showed Macbeth Duncan's blood on my hands – only it wasn't Macbeth standing there, it was my gentlewoman and the physician. I saw Macbeth. As I thrust out my hands to display the blood to him, the candle slipped out of my hand and my woman caught it, but I was already walking forward. I knelt and starting putting stuff all over my face. I was looking in a mirror and making myself up to be Queen. To be the very, very beautiful Queen.

Then I was rubbing, rubbing. 'Yet here's a spot.' 'Out, damned spot!' Each of those angle turns in the speech was a new picture. 'One: two', – the clock strikes, she's hearing the bell she signalled Macbeth with when everything was 'provided' – 'why then, 'tis time to do't.' And *we've got to do it*. The next thought that came – 'Hell is murky!' – was utterly bereft. She was using loss, the loss of him, the loss of the child. Without him she didn't know where to go. Hell is murky and she's lost her way; she doesn't know the way through.

Then all the old gestures began to echo what had gone before. 'Fie, my lord, fie! A soldier and afeard?' was very prim; 'What need we fear . . . none can call our power to accompt' was irritable and steely together – one can imagine that she said many times, '*We are untouchable!*' But the next picture pushes in – talk about untouchable! 'Yet who would have thought the old man to have had so much blood in him?' I was looking at Duncan's body again. Those Scottish castles have lots of very small stone rooms. It was easy to imagine one of those little bedchambers covered in blood from wall to wall.

I played a madness in this scene that I don't think has been there in other productions. It was a mind that had disintegrated into shards – that's how I imagined her – rather than a retrospective, reflective consideration of my life. I couldn't play that option. I tried a few times in rehearsals, but it didn't work. I felt this desolate child saying, 'We can do it – we can – no we can't – I've lost him. I've lost him!' A mind in shards.

On the 'Oh! Oh! Oh!' I collapsed on the floor. But then I pulled myself together, in queenly fashion, took my little pot of carmine, made up my lips with that queen-red lipstick, put my carmine away, looked down at my hand – and saw blood on my fingers! It was the carmine, but I *saw* Duncan's blood! I went berserk then and began scrabbling in the earth. I tried to rub the blood off the floor, but then the floor suddenly shot out – a plank in the boards shot forward – and this place was turning into a gallery built over hell!

Technically, one of the things I found useful was the idea that when the plank shot out, I had my battlement: I walked forward, out on the battlement, and I was going to throw myself over! That was the moment when I was going to kill myself – only I couldn't, and I retreated, pulling myself together, saying, 'Wash your hands; put on your nightgown.'

And then that last line, 'I tell you yet again, Banquo's buried, he cannot come out on's grave.' Adrian Noble gave me a note on that line: she's saying, 'No – please – this *can't* be happening,' she's trying to persuade herself, to hold their madness at bay. It's an absolute panic attack. She's shaking. '*Don't* say he's come out of his grave, because if we admit to that one, we're lost.'

But that's exactly what she was, lost, and these are Lady Macbeth's last lines in the play. The ravaged sleepwalker, showing only the vestiges of the golden girl she had been, recalled the witches' paradox, 'Fair is foul and foul is fair', for the beauty was defaced, and, in winning, Lady Macbeth lost everything. The murderer ended up a suicide. For Sinead Cusack, the end of Lady Macbeth's play was 'Lonely. So lonely. Utter desolation. I couldn't have done it in my twenties.'

4
Helena and Imogen: The Achievers

The most frustrating thing about playing Shakespeare's
women is having to dislodge the audience's preconceptions of who they are. Shakespeare's men don't
have 'reputations'. His women do. The men can be
compromised or compromising. The women can be
neither. The women have to be 'liked'. *Harriet*

Harriet Walter has in mind the roles that established her name at
the RSC, both of them heroines she tried to rescue from their
'reputations': Helena in *All's Well That Ends Well* (1981, directed by
Trevor Nunn) and Imogen in *Cymbeline* (1987, directed by Bill
Alexander).

'The Victorians gave Imogen the reputation that has stuck. They
loved her. She was their perfect fairy-tale-princess-as-wife, a role-
model for women in marriage.' So entrenched is this notion that even
today, even for some feminists, Imogen is still a patient Griselda,
resigned and passive, submissiveness personified. Helena's reputation
is fixed in an entirely different mould. *All's Well* has no stage history
worth mentioning before 1916, and it wasn't until the 1950s that it
began to be performed regularly at Stratford. This was partly because
of a historical antagonism towards Helena that labelled her immodest
and ambitious, predatory and sanctimonious at the same time. As
recently as 1981, despite the production's sympathetic reappraisal of
the character, one reviewer still saw in Harriet Walter's performance
'the martyr-bitch Helena'.

Helena has had some admirers. G. B. Shaw liked her even more than
he disliked Imogen. He saw Helena as a New Woman who predicted
Nora in *A Doll's House*, Imogen as an 'unspeakable person' in whom
'virtuous indignation is chronic'. Shaw's verdict on Helena was echoed
by another journalist a hundred years later. In 1981 James Fenton
fantasised about a Shakespeare who, ground down by 'years of catering
for tiresome actor-laddies', finally cut loose to write in Helena his 'best
female role'. She was 'the woman of the future for the actress of the
future'.

In Harriet Walter's experience most female reputations, including

Imogen's and Helena's, are quite simply wrong. Imogen docile, long-suffering? Helena scheming?

No. And no. Imogen is imperious, headstrong, fiery, temperamental. It's there in Shakespeare's text! She makes decisions quite hot-headedly. A lot of the time she practically looks through Pisanio – the faithful servant who believes in her when her husband doesn't and who saves her life. She bashes people aside quite arrogantly. But she's humbled. The experiences she has teach her humility.

And Helena: far from being a kind of devouring tiger-female, she's desperately tentative. She is indeed manipulative, but then Fate keeps encouraging her, telling her she's right. She's an opportunist whose opportunities are made by the gods. But she's always diffident. Again, that Helena, the one who's chancing her arm, is in the script. And she too is humbled.

The characteristic I find most prominent in each of them – maybe audiences don't expect this – is courage.

The two plays look like the products of quite different theatrical traditions. *Cymbeline* is one of Shakespeare's last works, a rambling chronicle that starts in Roman-conquest Britain, then cuts from kidnapped princes raised in Welsh caves to a Rome whose sexual mores belong to the Renaissance and Machiavelli. Imogen is Britain's princess, apparently King Cymbeline's only surviving child, and she has secretly married the noble but humbly born Posthumus. When the marriage is discovered, he is banished. In Italy, taunted by the lubricious schemer Iachimo, Posthumus wagers on Imogen's virtue. Persuaded by Iachimo that she has been unfaithful, Posthumus orders Pisanio to kill her. Instead, Pisanio disguises her in man's apparel and leads her to sanctuary in Wales. There she meets unknowingly her kidnapped brothers, who fight for Britain when an army is sent from Rome. The war assembles everyone: they discover their identities, marvel at a sceneful of miracles, and forgive each other.

All's Well That Ends Well is a sombre problem play that opens like *Hamlet* and proceeds like Chekhov before ending like the Book of Revelation. Helena, a poor physician's daughter and ward to the newly widowed Countess of Rossillion, is hopelessly in love with Bertram, the young Count. When he leaves Rossillion to take his place at Court, Helena follows him. She cures the King, miraculously, of an incurable disease and, offered any payment she chooses, asks for Bertram in marriage. Bertram spurns her. The King imposes his will and insists upon the marriage. But once it has taken place Bertram runs away to the wars with Parolles, a braggart misleader of youth, and sends Helena home with a taunting letter:

> When thou canst get the ring upon my finger, which never shall come off, and show me a child begotten of thy body that I am father to, then call me husband; but in such a 'then' I write a 'never'.

In Harriet's performance the two roles emerged as very distinct characters. Imogen's eyes flashed; Helena's, caught staring at Bertram, dropped. Imogen was irrepressible, her lines racing. Helena was hesitant, secretive, internal, her language broken. In some respects, though, Helena and Imogen were sisters, linked by the nature of the actress who played them.

I think I have been cast as an actress who can play suppressed emotion, who can insinuate hidden strengths. Helena and Imogen both have that in them. But they are also both women who are not frightened by competition, women who are taking responsibility for the lives they will lead. They are women who are proving something in a man's world: Imogen by cross-dressing, and being put through a test of virtue in a male situation; and Helena by taking on various properties of maleness, in decision-making, pursuing, wooing. Helena is perhaps Shakespeare's only heroine who achieves things in a male way without putting on trousers.

It is so seldom that women are tested in a masculine way. Male virtue is tested *actively*: men prove their honour, their virtue, by doing good deeds and fighting good battles, by challenging obstacles and learning from consequences: 'You made the right decision there or the wrong decision there, you won that battle, you treated those people well.' Female virtue is tested passively. Female virtue is a state of being, not doing: a woman *is* good. She doesn't have to *do* anything, but she has to *be* unsoiled, untainted, preferably a blonde, definitely a virgin.

It's men who have created this view of female virtue and have tied it up with chastity and virginity. It is they who determine that women should *be* but not *do*. But to be a woman is to want to test out the virtues of a human being under the same conditions as a man. And when I was playing Helena, I discarded that male criterion – a mere convenience! – that celebrates the woman 'as long as she's innocent and pure and I can worship her' but is disgusted by her when she gets her hands dirty and enters the male world. Helena gets her hands dirty. Helena demands to be judged by what she's done, how she's passed male tests, how generously she's used the knowledge she's acquired.

Helena was the first to teach me this. I confess to finding ideas like 'virtue', 'honour', 'chastity' – big concepts in Shakespeare – hard to get into. Helena showed me a way through that, which was to do with substituting the word 'integrity' – me being true to me, a sense of self, and honour inside yourself – for those inaccessible ideas of honour. Maybe this helps with someone like Isabella in *Measure for Measure*, if you replace 'chastity' with 'integrity'.

Imogen has the same quality of integrity, but the most important quality she shares with Helena is that they are both female achievers in a male world.

And it is because these seemingly incompatible plays both focus on women achievers that Harriet would urge them to be considered as a pair. For her, the process of discovering a role is a process of discarding, of uncovering the bare script.

First you have to clear away the heroine's reputation. Then you have to clear away the received idea about the character. Then you have to clear away the idea of character itself!

It was pointed out to me when I was rehearsing *Three Sisters* with John Barton that the term 'character' has only relatively recently acquired the meaning it has for us now. We tend to think of 'character' as something psychologically coherent or consistent, something that has a sub-text. Shakespeare doesn't seem to think of 'characters' like this. And you (actor, reader or audience) shouldn't make any prejudgement about what a 'character' is, whether she's one thing or another, brave/not brave, generous/not generous, virtuous/not virtuous. What you need to do is to understand her, get behind her, using the text as your only clue.

In a sense the character doesn't speak the text, the text 'speaks' the character. Through the movement of the verse, the rhythm of the speech, the confrontation with other characters, the echoing of ideas, the selection of certain words and the repetition of imagery, the mental and emotional life of the character is revealed.

You then play each scene or each beat, however contradictory, or however incompatible it seems with what has gone before or comes after. You play the moment for its integrity, for what it is. Then, by the end of the play, the character is an accumulation of all those separate moments.

If you concern yourself less with presentation and evaluation of a character, and allow your actor's instinct to respond to the music and the particularity of each word, if you trust Shakespeare whenever you're in doubt, you give yourself a chance of truly making the character yours. Then your individuality can give it more 'contemporary relevance' than an imposed interpretative construct.

When she began work on Helena, Harriet was determined to see the play fresh and allow the character to arrive as that 'accumulation of separate moments'. This meant beginning at the beginning, not, she says, 'at the end, like the critics do when they see Helena as a man-trap forcing Bertram – poor Bertram – into an unwanted marriage'. So she refused to start with the effects of Helena's ambition on Bertram. Instead, she began with 'an innocent reading of Helena's famous soliloquy, the one that ends the first scene of the play':

> Our remedies oft in ourselves do lie,
> Which we ascribe to heaven. The fated sky
> Gives us free scope, only doth backward pull
> Our slow designs when we ourselves are dull.
> What power is it which mounts my love so high,
> That makes me see, and cannot feed mine eye?
> The mightiest space in fortune nature brings
> To join like likes, and kiss like native things.
> Impossible be strange attempts to those
> That weigh their pains in sense, and do suppose
> What hath been cannot be. Who ever strove
> To show her merit that did miss her love?
> The King's disease – my project may deceive me,
> But my intents are fixed, and will not leave me.

This soliloquy epitomises what you might call the 'Helena music' of the play. It's cryptic, self-conscious, secretive. She's talking to the audience here, and she could come out and declare herself if she did have a confident strategy, if she were a schemer. She's got the freedom to say what she wants. But instead she remains undisclosed.

If you allow the verse to work on you instead of imposing yourself on it, what you find out about the rhythm of thought is that Helena here is very tentative. Every line is split half way so that the sense of the sentence is in the first half of the next line. You get the feeling of an impulse to keep explaining, as if she herself doesn't know quite what she's doing. She isn't declarative. The lines don't go 'statement, statement, statement', 'agenda, agenda, agenda'. They wind about. They are an assortment of riddle, wish-fulfilment, maxim and question. Even when she plucks 'the King's disease' out of the air, she still doesn't disclose a plan. It's still a kind of guess or stab in the dark. And Bertram isn't even mentioned in the speech.

When I came innocent to Helena's text, I had no trouble finding in the lines a woman who was very internal – dark, intense, the kind of woman who writes diaries. But one who was not sure of herself – whose lines kept exposing her tentativeness, her sense of, 'I know this is crazy. I know I'm mad. I will probably fail. But I'm going to try.'

It's not just individual speeches that expose Helena's lack of confidence, for, as Harriet points out, 'Other characters constantly undermine her, and the whole first scene seems structured to marginalise her.' It is composed of two actions, the leave-taking of Bertram followed by the leave-taking of Parolles. Helena, on stage throughout, is left alone, and speaks a soliloquy after each farewell.

As the play begins, Lafeu, the King's chief counsellor, has recently arrived at Rossillion to escort Bertram to Court. The Countess (Peggy Ashcroft in this production), solicitous of the King's health, bids her son adieu, while Bertram, anxious to be away, chafes. Helena is the topic of conversation, but she stands aside: 'Shakespeare puts her on the fringe of the action, a figure in black, weeping.'

Everyone thinks her tears are for her dead father, the famous physician who might have cured the King. When the Countess rebukes her tears as affected, Helena replies obscurely, 'I do affect a sorrow indeed, but I have it too,' a riddle that is explained when the stage clears, and she is left alone to reveal that her tears are not for her father but for her departing 'bright star', her idol, Bertram. In Harriet Walter's performance, obsessiveness combined with self-mockery in this first soliloquy:

> Th'ambition in my love thus plagues itself:
> The hind that would be mated by the lion
> Must die for love. Twas pretty, though a plague,
> To see him every hour, to sit and draw
> His archèd brows, his hawking eye, his curls
> In our heart's table . . .
> But now he's gone, and my idolatrous fancy
> Must sanctify his relics.

Helena is interrupted by Parolles who, as Helena declares, is 'a notorious liar . . . a great way fool, solely a coward'. Because he's idolised by Bertram she freely tolerates him, but she knows the man is a fop made by his tailor. In this production he entered festooned with white scarves like a military parade ground draped in bunting. Standing next to Helena, his appearance mocked her sober mourning just as his repartee mocked her elegiac self-absorption.

> *Parolles* Save you, fair Queen!
> *Helena* And you, monarch!
> *Parolles* No.
> *Helena* And no.
> *Parolles* Are you meditating on virginity?

Helena does not duck his vulgarity. Wittily, she engages with him, jibing at his military pretensions whilst soliciting military advice as to how a virgin might adopt a 'warlike resistance' so as to 'barricade' herself against 'the enemy', man. Parolles talks and talks and talks; Helena's replies grow shorter and shorter until she finally explodes with lines Harriet describes as 'one of Helena's uncrackable code speeches'.

It seems like a hymn to virginity, but it is so oblique that Parolles has to interrupt her. The exchange ends with more quips and Parolles' farewell: 'Get thee a good husband, and use him as he uses thee.' Alone again, Helena begins the second soliloquy, 'Our remedies oft in ourselves do lie . . .'

Harriet thinks that Shakespeare was using Parolles as the bridge that conducts Helena from inaction to action.

Shakespeare structures the scene so wonderfully, with those two soliloquies punctured by Parolles' entrance. Parolles is such a *release*. Helena is so intense at the end of the first one: it's as if the skin of a balloon is stretched tight across her emotion, to bursting point. And Parolles lets all the air out of the balloon.

It's often difficult to figure out why, logically, Shakespeare puts something in a scene. You can't analyse it. Something might work by analogy – it reflects something – or then again it might work by association: it makes you think of something else, or it connects to something that's coming. Parolles, here, works in lots of ways.

In his terms, Helena *is* 'meditating on virginity': she is, for the time being, buying into the male concept of male/female relation-ships that, in the second soliloquy, she is going to reject when she decides to go after a husband. But she's also instinctively rejecting that double patronising of women implied in 'Save you, fair Queen'.

'Queen' puns with 'quean', meaning whore, and Helena isn't accepting either male mythologising of women – turning them into 'queens' – or male reductionism, making them all whores. That's very interesting because other men in the play have this habit of impudence with Helena. They keep implying she's a whore. And maybe that's Shakespeare playing with the conventional role-models available to women who are achievers: either they're angels sent with miracles, or they're sexual workers getting things done that way. Anyway, in a later scene Lafeu cracks dirty jokes about her to the King before they meet and when he leaves them he says he's 'Cressid's uncle', i.e. he's a pander, she's the prostitute. Parolles is dealing in the same innuendo here.

But Parolles also makes Helena feel like an attractive woman. The raillery is sexy. It shows her as someone not weepy but someone witty, *sexy*. And it shows one of Helena's best traits, the way she can speak the right language for the right person – apart from the fact that she can't open her mouth when she's with Bertram. She can't even say goodbye to him! But with everybody else, she can mix with them and win people over. With Parolles she can crack dirty jokes and flirt; with the Countess in the next scene she can be pure and passionate; with the King, discursive, argumentative, persuasive.

But for Harriet, the scene also has a very bitter edge.

It goes back to what I said about everybody being familiar, *insolent* to Helena. They can all be derisive, and their scepticism about her power is going to take the form of sexual taunting. She's a kind of nonentity, a poor physician's daughter: I played her with a bunch of keys at my waist like a housekeeper. Shakespeare gives her absolutely no room for self-confidence. In this scene, even a fool can humiliate her. And I think that's the beat her soliloquy, 'Our remedies oft in ourselves do lie', *begins* with. When she is confronted with scepticism, derision, Helena gets tough. Before Parolles came in she was in despair. His scoffing does something. The scene is a bridge from one kind of emotion to the other, in which tentativeness is now balanced by resolve.

Trevor Nunn, Harriet's director, encouraged her to explore both Helena's hesitancy and her tenacity.

He started me out with two character points about Helena. He felt that the unpopularity of the play stemmed from the fact that Helena is a *woman* who gets what she's after. She *is* manipulative; she *is* obsessive; and she *seems* to have no sense of humour. She's very intense, so she's not someone you'd like to have at a dinner party. But he took the line that if we are to follow the journey of this woman throughout the evening, we cannot be alienated by her. We must at least understand her.

So he wanted a sympathetic Helena. Hence the two character points. The first was that she should be self-critical and apologetic, not triumphant or smugly self-vindicating. The second was that where she had signs of a sense of humour, of self-irony, we should bring that out. He believed these traits would stand her in good stead when she does things in the play that the audience don't approve of. Like 'pursuing' Bertram, although, as you'll see in a moment, she doesn't really 'pursue' him at all.

In the play it is clearly the case that Helena constantly wins people over: the Countess, the King, the Widow in Florence. Helena has this wonderful capacity almost instantly to win the hearts of other people. And Trevor wanted the audience to see this.

Nunn also helped Harriet's performance with a shrewd casting decision.

Mike Gwilym was Bertram. As an actor, Mike can put over brooding qualities: a slight misogynism, surliness, Strindbergian intensity. He glowers. And he was terribly attractive to Helena, but not soft, not yielding, not kind. Between Helena and Bertram there was the attraction of strange metals.

In Trevor's scenario, Bertram had funny dreams about Helena. She's someone who's been raised in the household but is only the daughter of a family retainer. So he's somehow disturbed by her because he *mustn't* love her. He doesn't like the effect she has on him so he cuts her out. The bigger influence in Bertram's life is the older man, Parolles, who's a wastrel, a braggart-buffoon. *Everybody* sees through Parolles. Someone calls him a 'window of lattice'. But not Bertram, because Parolles appeals to his ego and makes him feel like a man. Parolles is a kind of father-substitute – Bertram's father has just died – except that Parolles doesn't fit Bertram's world. He's a totally unsuitable companion. But he represents exploration, Bertram's chance to break out of expectations. It's like the Hal/Falstaff syndrome in the *Henry IV* plays, or like a public schoolboy who runs off with a rock'n'roll band.

When Parolles gets his comeuppance in Act IV, what Trevor

wanted was for Bertram to be completely broken. The edifice of his ego shatters and makes him reappraise his values so that he has room to build up again, in humility, respect for a woman, to see how wrong he's been about people. Trevor wanted him to admit his love for Helena and to begin to grow up, again like Hal rejecting the questionable male values of Falstaff to take on marriage to Katherine. In our production Bertram's youth was emphasised; at one point someone handed him a cigarette and he took a drag and coughed. That was to indicate that this man had places to go, lessons to learn; he wasn't someone established, who would never change.

Mike didn't completely conform to Trevor's scenario. And he signalled his independence pretty early on. He deliberately avoided watching too many rehearsals of Helena's scenes for fear of becoming too sympathetic towards her.

Nunn gave his actors a strong frame for their performances. By setting the production a few years before the First World War in an Edwardian twilight of elegance and Empire, he provided a context for exploring the obsessions and inhibitions, the tensions between personal initiatives and obedience to authority, that are built into the play. The set looked like a cross between Paddington Station and a conservatory at Kew. The garden at Rossillion contained wicker chairs and potted ferns in Chinese pots; leather armchairs turned the space into the Court. Chopinesque reveries accompanied scene changes. In Harriet's opinion, none of this detail was gratuitous:

Trevor's great skill as a director is to pick up what every actor is doing and use it. He gives you the physical framework, the *space*, in which your performance can enact the emotion that is being released by the text. He puts in your hands what you need to objectify the feelings or the ideas the text is throwing out – he gives you a handkerchief to knot when your character needs one.

What Trevor did for me was to 'place' Helena's tentativeness. He gave me a way of *demonstrating* that idea. In II, i, for example, Helena appears at Court to cure the King. My first instincts in early rehearsals told me she wasn't at all confident, she didn't think it was going to work, and I showed that by how hesitantly she entered. Trevor picked up that hesitancy and extended it: he had me *leave* the scene. I had to be summoned back.

Once again, the scene itself gives Helena no grounds for confidence.

She is introduced to the King with a smutty joke that implies she is a whore, which clearly throws her off balance. She speaks first a half-line, then two metrically short lines, as if trying to recover composure:

> Ay, my good lord.
> Gerard de Narbon was my father,
> In what he did profess, well found.

When the King shows not just scepticism but contempt for her ability to cure him, Harriet's Helena didn't argue.

I got my suitcase, put on my coat, and made for the door. 'My duty then shall pay me for my pains./I will no more enforce mine office on you . . .' was my exit line. I genuinely thought, 'This is crazy, what I'm trying to do is crazy – and I've got to get out!' But as I left, the King tossed over his shoulder: 'What at full I know, thou knowest no part;/I knowing all my peril, thou no art,' meaning, 'You don't know anything.' That stops Helena in her tracks. Her response is, 'Wait a minute! I *am* going to try this.' So having left the scene, she comes back into it, and on a higher plane, a higher energy level, because she's been challenged. She commits herself to trying. It's as though her own integrity is at stake, and that's more important to her than any vilification or ridicule she might get for attempting it. She has to be true to herself.

Similarly, in II, ii, the scene when Helena has cured the King and is granted her desire to choose a husband, the production exposed the fragility of the moment rather than celebrating her ostensible triumph. It was staged as an elimination ball. Helena entered transformed, in an Empire gown, elbow gloves and jewels, dancing with the miraculously restored King. As the King assembled his wards – the men whose marriage he has in gift – the stage filled with high-spirited masculinity. These courtiers danced formation patterns before Helena and each time the music stopped she eliminated a candidate, until it came to Bertram. He was the winner. But he didn't want marriage, and he didn't want Helena. Harriet Walter feels that the scene was delicately judged: 'The formation dance expressed something scenically about the emotional truth of the text at that moment.'

Nunn also encouraged her to develop that other aspect of Helena, the tenaciousness that showed itself in her conviction 'that she is right to love this man Bertram, that it is her destiny, that the Fates are approving and abetting her actions'. For Harriet,

Helena is right: our remedies do lie in ourselves. And the 'fated sky', 'heaven', keeps agreeing with her! She wins everybody over. She gets the Countess's approval, both to go to Court and to love Bertram, in I, iii. She can be forgiven for believing that her mission is blessed. In II, i she performs the miracle that allows her to have her wish answered: she cures the King.

It's the most magic scene of all. She works a miracle: the disease is incurable and she cures him. *She* does it. Is it the medicine she's brought, her father's secret remedy? I don't think so. I think it's Helena. She starts out so unsure, apologetic, not 'I have this whole scene taped and I've come to twist you around my little finger,' but, 'I haven't got a plan. I'm busking this one. I'm going to try my best, but there's no guarantee.'

But then when the King persists in his death-wish, something goes rigid in Helena. A chasm opens up between two people, one who has given up on life and wants to die, the other who has faith in life, a reason to live, a drive and a great determination that is activated by confronting a man who is content to die. He wants to give up; she refuses to let him go. Both people's philosophies offend the other's. She declares for life: 'I just won't buy this! You can't throw life away!' And it's infectious – she taps his last drop of wanting to live. Her vigour literally invigorates him.

Helena cures the Court's scepticism too: she has performed a miracle, and becomes an object of veneration as a result.

This makes Bertram's repudiation at the end of the elimination ball all the more difficult.

Helena thought it was class that stood between her and Bertram. She finds out at the ball that he doesn't love her, that nothing would induce him to marry her even if the King raised her to the rank of princess. This is the first time she has to face that fact. She's done everything in her power to bring things to this point, but, confronted by Bertram's loathing for her, she has no wish to proceed any further. She says to the King,

> That you are well restored, my lord, I'm glad.
> Let the rest go.

I left the ballroom and had to be dragged back in. When the King brings us together I want the ground to open up; it's gone desperately wrong, and this is not what I want. But now male pride has taken over: the King's honour is at stake. He has been defied, so he forces the marriage through. At that moment both Helena and Bertram are victims of his power and hate it.

Helena is desperately shy after the marriage, when Bertram summons her to send her home (II,v). I think she embarrasses him with her fulsomeness:

> Sir, I can nothing say
> But that I am your most obedient servant . . .
> And ever shall
> With true observance seek to eke out that
> Wherein toward me my homely stars have failed
> To equal my great fortune.

Talk about apologetic! He keeps trying to make her stop talking, but she still doesn't leave. Then she stammers out that she wants something and he has to ask her three times what it is. Finally she says, 'Strangers and foes do sunder and not kiss' – typically cryptic, she's saying she wants to kiss him goodbye. He replies, 'I pray you, stay not, but in haste to horse.' In our production he didn't kiss her; he couldn't give her any hope.

Sent home to Rossillion with the assurance that he will follow in a day or two, Helena opens Bertram's letter telling her he won't return home until she's dead: 'Till I have no wife I have nothing in France.' Harriet believes that Bertram means what he says.

And I also believe what Helena does next. She reads Bertram's impossible challenge – 'When thou canst get the ring upon my finger, which never shall come off, and show me a child begotten of thy body that I am father to . . .' – and sees it as impossible. She responds with a very pragmatic solution: she decides to leave France. She says it all in the soliloquy at the end of III, ii:

> Poor lord, is't I
> That chase thee from thy country, and expose
> Those tender limbs of thine to the event
> Of the none-sparing war? . . .
> No, come thou home, Rossillion . . .
> I will be gone:
> My being here it is that holds thee hence.
> Shall I stay here to do't? No, no . . .
> I will be gone.

Helena doesn't pursue Bertram to Florence. She believes that as soon as she's gone he'll come home. She's going to be a nun, a pilgrim: '*Mea culpa*. I've gone too far. I didn't realise. I'd better stop this game.' I believe all that is quite genuine. Helena is in love with Bertram, and she sees now that she's trapped him. He's going to fight a war. He may get killed. And she understands his point of view. She only wanted to chance her arm because she thought it was class that stood between them.

So when she gets to Florence – my God, he's there! It's incredible. There has to be something in the Fates again colluding with her destiny. This is very important: the usual assumption is that she chases him to the wars, but she doesn't. Helena doesn't manipulate that meeting. It's coincidental, her bumping into the very troops where Bertram is flirting with Diana. Shakespeare frequently engineers coincidences that have some kind of fatalistic drive behind them – like Imogen meeting her brothers in the cave in Wales – and I think we should respect Fate here instead of suspecting Helena. Her desire has been to get away from Bertram, and now here he is! So she thinks, once again, somehow, some way, this relationship has got to be right . . .

Bertram has fallen for Diana, the Widow's daughter, whom all the soldiers know to be invincibly chaste, yet he persists in his attempts to seduce her. Seeing an opportunity, Helena approaches the Widow with a proposal. She 'starts to mix in the market-place' – Harriet's phrase for the negotiations between the two women.

Helena makes a bargain with the Widow that will enable her to win Bertram's impossible challenge – getting his ring and 'getting' his child. It means she has to plot and manipulate, but she thinks, 'I've got to do it. Fate has dealt me this hand; I've got to play this card. I'm in it up to my neck!'

> Take this purse of gold,
> And let me buy your friendly help thus far,
> Which I will over-pay, and pay again
> When I have found it.

There's something about that money exchange with the Widow that I found expressive of getting your hands dirty. Helena got into that language of exchange, of buying and selling *with Italians*! She can cross a lot of borders and barriers, impelled by what she wants at the end, and by the final scene she's learned something about herself.

And Bertram has too. I think that's what the Parolles plot is all about.

To force callow Bertram to face the fact that the man he hero-worships is made of clay, the regiment practises an elaborate deception upon Parolles, ambushing him, persuading him he's been captured by the enemy, interrogating him blindfolded. Parolles not only gives away intelligence secrets but slanders his comrades, including Bertram. When the blindfold is lifted, they face each other and both are exposed. Harriet sees this moment as crucial to an understanding of the relationship between Helena and Bertram, and the resolution of the play.

The Parolles plot isn't just a comic interlude or social comment. It's a contribution – it must be – to Bertram's understanding of himself and his system of values, to make him reappraise them and be open to the possibility of what Helena is. Bertram's humiliation here is a counterpart to Helena's in the ballroom: in the last act he's exposed to more and more shame. But humiliation leads to self-discovery. Both Bertram and Helena receive a hefty blow to their self-confidence and both get dirty in the world – so that at the end Helena is saying, 'We've both lived a bit, we're both soiled articles, but I think you'll find we've got a chance.'

Bertram enters the last scene believing, as everyone does, that Helena is dead, prepared to salvage his reputation with the King by marrying another bride of the King's choice. He speaks ruefully of Helena as 'she whom all men praised, and whom myself,/ Since I have lost, have loved.' Reproaching himself for misjudging her, for thinking of her as 'the dust that did offend' his eye, he pulls a ring off his finger to send to his new bride. It is the ring Bertram thinks Diana gave him in bed, but the King recognises it as the one he gave Helena, and concludes that Bertram has murdered her. Bertram is dumbfounded.

Diana appears and he slanders her as an impudent 'gamester' of the camp. Then Parolles is produced; he confirms Diana's story. But then Diana cavils with the evidence produced in her own defence. The ring is not hers, nor did she give it to Bertram. The King, infuriated by her apparent deviousness, now threatens her with arrest. Diana defends herself with a riddle. Bertram is

> guilty and he is not guilty;
> He knows I am no maid, and he'll swear to't;
> I'll swear I am a maid, and he knows not.

And she sends her mother, the Widow, to 'fetch my bail'. The doors open. Helena, alive and evidently pregnant, stands there.

She enters not with a flourish, not with a triumphant sense of 'Gotcha!', but self-critically, knowing she's been devious, knowing she's engineered things by playing a trick on Bertram and going to bed with him in the dark, admitting that it's not clean and wonderful and that she's not proud of it.

Trevor Nunn felt that Helena was a redeemer, a woman whose faith and integrity were going to save Bertram from his callowness. He thought Bertram would be humbled by her tenacity, would see her as his only hope at that point – both metaphorically and literally, because Bertram, by his lies, is well and truly caught in a corner. Trevor wanted an optimistic ending.

Now the fact that Bertram's caught in a corner is one thing; it doesn't necessarily mean that that is how Helena wanted things to turn out. I feel that she would have liked something different, but she can see that everything has got messy, and since that's the case all she can say is, 'It's you and me, boy; there's nowhere else to go, so let's try to make a success of it.'

I couldn't relate to Trevor's redeeming saint. I felt Helena was much too compromised by the events of the play – and she knew it – to play at redemption. I couldn't make redemption out of the messiness.

Mike Gwilym resisted the happy ending. I think he wanted the 'dust that did offend' speech to be a piece of propaganda, designed to get back in with everybody, to cut his losses. Trevor wanted it to be sincere: Bertram had loved Helena all along but discovered it too late. Mike wanted the ending to be bitter for Bertram.

So we had a kind of three-cornered hat at the end, but I sided with Mike in performance because the last thing I wanted was anything sentimental. At the same time I thought, 'You don't put people through three and a half hours of torment about two people you don't care about, who are going to end up saying, "Life is going to be terrible".' So our play ended on a real knife-edge that contained various possibilities – Mike's bitterness, Trevor's hope, and my circumscribed hope – something that was workable but not easy or pretty.

We didn't kiss at the end. We walked out of the play side by side, just our fingertips touching. Parolles' line, 'Simply the thing I am will make me live,' applied to Bertram and Helena in our production, and the play's title could be read as quite ironic. We saw what happens in the play as resembling what happens in real life: that's what makes it a 'problem' play. It's the idea spoken by one of those unnamed soldiers, and it informs the whole play:

> The web of our life is of a mingled yarn, good and ill together: our virtues would be proud, if our faults whipped them not; and our crimes would despair if they were not cherished by our virtues.

It's a very mingled ending. When Helena appears – from the dead, they believe! – the stage shows a miracle. Again, it's a metaphor, but it's also literal: she's transformed, she's pregnant. And there has to be a kind of awe – like the awe you need to believe in the last act of *Cymbeline*: the characters on stage have to have a capacity to be in awe of the workings of Fate.

You can't be a cynic to play Shakespeare. You have to have that room in you for spiritual uplift. In *All's Well*, and even more so in *Cymbeline*, you really have to believe in the possibility of forgiveness and reconciliation. You have to believe that forgiveness wasn't just wishful thinking on the part of a tired old man, and that reconciliation is just as possible in real life as the dark alternatives.

For Harriet, it's this sense of awe that lifts female achievement into a metaphysical area. Men may make history by winning wars, but in her winning of a husband Helena achieves something higher: she exposes the secret workings of Fate, humanity's relationship to the gods. In *Cymbeline* it's a man who is visited by the gods, while the play's politics start with a woman. But by the end, the awe centres on Imogen, and once again the domestic details of her achievement, her tenacity in passing male tests of virtue, are transformed by wonder into revelation. Imogen is a woman 'who has had miraculous things dealt to her by the gods'.

Harriet hesitates to sound 'too astrological' about *Cymbeline* but she does think that it has a message for today's audiences.

I think it is incredibly relevant right now because of current ways of thinking, both in politics and in more mystical areas. We're at a point in history when it's possible that rather than looking down towards the inevitable global holocaust, we might just do a complete U-turn instead. Human beings might not have an in-built self-destruct mechanism; they may have the intelligence to see what they are doing and use that same intelligence to prevent it.

It's happening in environmental politics; it's happening in summit meetings. Of course, many people are cynical about motives, but what no one would deny is the universal desire that the globe should survive. We've got to the very worst point, and when you get to that point you say, 'Now we could turn round.' It's all to do with political will, and a recognition of the interdependence of our fates.

That, I think, is what happens in *Cymbeline*. At the end the King says, 'Although the victor, we submit to Caesar.' We've won, but we'll concede. When Posthumus forgives Iachimo, Cymbeline says: 'We'll learn our freeness of a son-in-law:/Pardon's the word to all.' What they are doing is demonstrating the will to save themselves; it's a positive, intelligent choice for survival rather than doom. They have the choice to remain intractable and to feel that as long as they beat their enemy he can go under without another thought. Instead, they choose to see events globally: if the enemy goes down, they all go down.

Cymbeline starts with everyone throwing up nationalistic barriers. The Britons refer to Rome as 'drug-damned Italy', and the Italians see us as 'dull Britain'. When Imogen thinks she is betrayed by Posthumus she says, 'My lord, I fear,/Has forgot Britain' – she identifies *herself* with Britain. Everything is seen in terms of our nation. But then as the play goes on, and the confusions and contradictions intensify, the categories prove to be pretty ir-relevant: in Italy there is both an Iachimo and a Caius Lucius (one iniquitous, the other noble); in Britain there is both a Cloten and an Imogen: one a poltroon, the other a bright star.

I think Imogen's journey can be most clearly identified with the journey of the play, but for all the characters there's some kind of falling away of individual boxes so that the final discovery is that they are all one family, and the gods are over their heads. Shakespeare has to introduce two stage devices to make that revelation happen. He brings on the gods, something outside of us that will focus our common humanity, and he provides us with scapegoats: the wicked Queen and her bad son Cloten, who act as a purge for our society, making it possible for us to trust each other.

Ultimately the play throws human beings back on themselves – it makes people look at each other without their boxes and wonder whether one is much better than the other. That's what Posthumus does when he's faced by Iachimo at the end. All the characters go through that *mea culpa*, and through self-criticism, but instead of indulging it or growing bitter, they look at someone across the room who used to be their enemy and say, 'We might as well shake hands.'

That phrase, 'falling away of boxes', defines a common pattern of experience in *Cymbeline*. For Harriet's Imogen, the falling away process stemmed from a position of arrogance. In secretly marrying Posthumus, the Princess Royal had asserted her will. Harriet saw this as rash – like the marriage in *Romeo and Juliet* – and politically astute at the same time.

The scenario I adopted to explain what had happened just before the play begins – the clandestine marriage – was that Imogen and Posthumus, in quite an arrogant way, saw themselves as representing everything that is good about Britain. The two of them had been raised together, and nurtured together in this opinion of themselves, by Cymbeline. But Cymbeline himself has been corrupted. The evil Queen, Imogen's step-mother, is pulling him back, and he is now no more than an inept figure-head.

The idea that Imogen should espouse, literally and spiritually, Cloten, the Queen's obtuse but pernicious son, instead of Posthumus, is a warping of her integrity. To marry Cloten would corrupt the British line. So she takes the decision on herself: she saw what was coming, that it was on the cards she was going to be forced into a marriage with Cloten, and she acted to pre-empt it. She thought, 'Right, I'll marry Posthumus and that way I can't marry Cloten. It'll end in a terrible eruption, but I'll do it.'

And when it does explode, Imogen points out to her father that 'It is your fault that I have loved Posthumus:/You bred him as my playfellow.' Imogen seems to be asking, 'What's happened to you?' She believes it's up to her to put him right; she's tough in that way.

But she is also heir to the throne of Britain, and a decision to marry is not simply personal and romantic, it is also political. Harriet's Imogen, though fearless, was also ultimately naïve and, paradoxically, it was her frank sexuality that exposed her.

She's a rebel. She has deceived her father. She has defied her King. She has taken the law into her own hands and is going to stick with the decision she's made and thwart everybody's attempts to make her bend. She's a very courageous, certain person. She's a decision-maker. She's been bred to think of herself as a decision-maker.

Interestingly, Imogen is the only one of Shakespeare's cross-dressing women who doesn't herself decide to dress as a boy: the idea is put to her by Pisanio as a fairly routine act of caution. But as soon as he suggests it she jumps at it, saying, 'This attempt/I am soldier to, and will abide it with/A prince's courage.' It's as though she has a brother in her, who's never been allowed to come out. When she puts on men's clothes it's as though she knows there's a prince in them, and she embraces with great alacrity the opportunity it offers to test her male political will.

But she is also a *married* woman, who has slept with her husband. She is not a virgin. And while in some ways her 'knowing' makes her sexually frank, in other ways it exposes her vulnerabilities. There's an analogy to be drawn with Desdemona and Hermione, both married women, warm and friendly, both slandered in the mind of a jealous man who puts a pornographic construction on their generous caring for another person. For a woman to show any warmth towards a man is frequently seen as a sexual come-on.

That happens in I, vii, when Iachimo arrives at Court bringing a letter from banished Posthumus. Her generosity spills over and makes Imogen a dupe in the end because she's so willing to believe good of both Posthumus and Iachimo. It can be seen by Iachimo – and by some members of the audience – as a sexual invitation, and I deliberately play her as warm and sensual, because I can see good reasons for her to be friendly. She's starved of any news of Posthumus, starved of any contact with him, so she doesn't want this man Iachimo, who has actually spoken with Posthumus, to go away.

But as Harriet points out, it is Imogen's sexual experience with Posthumus that also makes her vulnerable in the scene. Eagerly she welcomes Iachimo and asks for news of Posthumus:

> Continues well my lord his health, beseech you?
> Is he disposed to mirth? I hope he is.

Iachimo reports that Posthumus is not just 'disposed to mirth' but that he's 'gamesome'; he's known in Rome as 'the Briton reveller'. To this Imogen responds simply: 'My lord, I fear,/Has forgot Britain.'
  She concludes that she has been betrayed.

Although Posthumus and Imogen had been brought up together and were quite trusting of one another as long as their relationship was platonic and brotherly/sisterly, as soon as they entered the treacherous region of sexuality and became sexual partners, they became strangers in some way. Though they had known one another from birth, that didn't stop them believing the worst of one another. Manipulated by Iachimo, they both fall prey to sexual jealousy. They are suddenly thrown into that area of what you might call cosmic torment between the sexes. And it's the archetypal man in Posthumus who responds to the archetypal woman in Imogen when he makes that archetypal speech about women in II, v.

> Is there no way for men to be but women
> Must be half-workers?. . .
>   Could I find out
> The woman's part in me! For there's no motion
> That tends to vice in man, but I affirm
> It is the woman's part. . .

In rehearsal, Harriet listened to Posthumus' invective, and while part of her was troubled by the experience, another part reacted philosophically, for, after all, Posthumus had got it wrong.

Actors get very defensive of their own characters: they identify with them, and so to be sitting in the rehearsal room hearing yourself talked about as he does, unable to intervene, is terribly distressing. Posthumus mistrusts her so totally! And on what grounds?

But then, they both mistrust. Posthumus gets punished hugely for mistrusting Imogen, but in I, vii Imogen, too, believed Iachimo's slanders and suggestions, even though she soon repented of it: 'I do condemn mine ears that have/So long attended thee.' In this first test of separation, we both fail, because we're faced with the thing we most value and most fear losing, so we almost *jump* to believe our fears. We expected it, really.

And it's not because I have doubts about Posthumus' character, or that he has doubts about mine, but that in some kind of abstract psychology that excludes individual cases, it is shrewd to have a cosmic male fear of women – because women inevitably betray men – and a cosmic female fear of men – because men invariably betray women. And because this particular man and this particular woman are separated, they can't any longer remember that it's *Imogen* (not 'women'), it's *Posthumus* (not 'men') that they're talking about.

The most important thing about Posthumus' soliloquy is that he's wrong; Imogen is not unfaithful. The entire diatribe is based on a fallacy. And the audience knows it when he speaks the soliloquy. So the speech says something about Posthumus, but nothing at all about Imogen or about women!

Imogen recovers from her momentary doubts about Posthumus almost immediately, but the poison injected in Posthumus has penetrated to the quick. From Rome he sets in motion the plan to have her killed. Pisanio, the loyal servant, takes her to the appointed place but instead of killing her, hands her men's clothing.

Dressed as a man, Imogen is pulled into the war that is sweeping across Britain. She is found weeping beside a headless corpse she thinks is Posthumus and is adopted by the Roman General Caius Lucius. The woman who thinks of herself as 'Britain' is beleaguered even as Britain is invaded. Is *Cymbeline* an allegory? Harriet Walter resists that idea vigorously.

Shakespeare isn't writing schematically: 'Imogen represents this' and 'Posthumus represents that', and then requiring us to refer to a bigger structure. He always blurs the edges of any scheme we try to set up. But he *is* bringing the twin themes of war and love into terrible proximity, and he's asking his audience to think about the politics of both.

What, then, is *Cymbeline* about? Harriet gives some unexpected answers.

One of the most important themes in the play is to do with service. It centres on the Pisanio figure: even as a servant, you can make choices. You have your duty, your menial position. But if you're given bad orders you shouldn't carry them out.

This is a test that Imogen faces too. As the dutiful daughter of the King, Imogen should comply with his order that she marry the corrupt Cloten. But she refuses. She thinks differently. And she's proved right by the events of the play. Although Posthumus is 'base-born' and Cloten the son of the Queen, she perceives that marriage to Posthumus is virtuous, to Cloten depraved. She preserves her integrity. Just as Pisanio preserves his integrity when he responds to Posthumus' command, 'If it be so to do good service, never/Let me be counted serviceable.'

There's always a choice. As Posthumus himself ironically says at the end, when he thinks Pisanio has carried out his order:

> Every good servant does not all commands:
> No bond but to do just ones.

A man can keep his integrity and say 'No'. And I think the play is saying, 'Stick with it, do what you know is right, and the gods will work it out.' I wish that were true in real life . . .

The other theme that pervades the play is more pessimistic. It has to do with characters' over-readiness to believe badly of each other. It obviously runs through the Posthumus/Imogen story but it is also central to Belarius, the right-hand officer to the King who was falsely accused of treason and banished and who stole the royal infants. He didn't have a trial; somebody managed to persuade Cymbeline on pretty flimsy evidence that a friend he trusted implicitly was confederate with the Romans! In all these cases, because the characters are ready to believe in the thing they most fear, they don't examine the evidence too closely. They respond, 'I knew it!' because it's what they had always dreaded.

Fear and despair are the vices, courage and hope the virtues of *Cymbeline*. The will to believe makes you keep going, even though all the events are against you. And in this play, you're rewarded for it.

That summarises Imogen's journey through the play, and Harriet points to III, iv as epitomising her character:

It's her last scene as a woman, and it contains a lot of what Imogen is. Essential Imogen comes out here, partly for the simple reason that she thinks she's confronting death. She summons up everything in herself.

She had thought of Posthumus and herself as representing something, sharing something in their hearts. Her brothers have been kidnapped, so it's up to her to hold on to that spirit of what is noble and good. Her father has lost it: he's gone down a dark alley with the wicked Queen.

And now, suddenly, it looks as if Posthumus has too. He has 'forgot Britain'. She knows that he can't believe she's false: when Pisanio hands her the letter accusing her of adultery, it still never crosses her mind that he could actually believe she would be unfaithful, so it must be that's he gone off with someone else, some Roman courtesan. Some 'jay of Italy' has lured him away. That's an example of Imogen's natural arrogance: she doesn't say, 'Posthumus has betrayed me,' but 'Some Roman' – everything she doesn't understand, everything that threatens her is 'Roman' – 'has betrayed *him*!'

Who's left to represent Britain? Only me. But 'only me' is still a big me! All the passions in this scene proclaim a big me. Big fury, big contempt, big grief, big indignation. When Pisanio meekly says that since he'd received Posthumus' command to kill her, 'I have not slept one wink,' she snaps back, 'Do't, and to bed then.' She describes herself as 'stale, a garment out of fashion' with Posthumus; 'And, for I am richer than to hang by the walls,/I must be ripp'd.' When she thinks she has been betrayed she exclaims, 'Men's vows are women's traitors.' She speaks of what she has done for Posthumus as 'no act of common passage, but/A strain of rareness'.

But then comes a point in the scene when she loses her faith in the whole concept of Britain.

> Hath Britain all the sun that shines? Day, night,
> Are they not but in Britain? I' the world's volume
> Our Britain seems as of it, but not in't;
> In a great pool, a swan's nest. Prithee, think
> There's livers out of Britain.

This is her turning point. Her disillusionment about Britain is a kind of shaking off of unquestioned values which throws her back on to herself. In this moment she sees that her integrity is still intact. She still exists: she can forget Posthumus, rip up his letters, expunge him from her heart, repudiate his corruption, and stand alone, without him for the first time ever – and survive. There is a great sense of herself. And the challenge of finding out what that self consists of: what is the heart of me if you strip everything away? My crown, my power, my position, my ideals, my husband. And from now on, even my sexual identity. What is *me*?

That's what it means to be a female achiever in these plays. It's not about getting a man, 'achieving' a husband. It's about finding out what your *self* consists of.

5
Rosalind: Iconoclast in Arden

'So this is the forest of Arden.' Three footsore travellers stand surveying exile. But what are they looking at? What *is* Arden? Not Epping Forest, that's for sure. *Juliet*

Juliet Stevenson had seen several productions of *As You Like It* before Adrian Noble approached her to play Rosalind in 1985, and she was impatient with interpretations that make the play seem safe, 'a rural romp in an Arden full of polystyrene logs', a 'celebration of the status quo that doesn't seem to be questioning anything'. For her, Arden is 'a metaphor, a landscape of the imagination and a realm of possibility, a place where gender definitions can be turned on their heads'.

I'd always suspected that there's a much more dangerous play in *As You Like It*. A subversive play, one that challenges notions of gender, that asks questions about the boundaries and qualities of our 'male' and 'female' natures. I'd heard these extraordinary arcs of thought from Rosalind, who says such radical things about love and its possibilities. And I got snatches of a wonderful relationship between two women, Celia and Rosalind. There's no real parallel to their journey anywhere in Shakespeare. I had never seen this friendship fully explored.

Fiona Shaw was cast as Celia; the friendship became central to the performance. Arden, too, was re-explored. This production saw the forest as 'a symbolist landscape' – Juliet's phrase – 'a venue for self-discovery and transformation':

The play is about love, love in all its forms. The love of an old shepherd for a young shepherd. The love of one girl for another. The love of a poet for a shepherdess. The love of an old servant for his master, and his master for him. It's about all those people. It's about Touchstone loving Audrey – that gloriously *impossible* partnership, that turns out to be possible.

Arden is the realm of that possibility. I don't think it's a real place, somewhere you can take a day trip to and look at the leaves and pick mushrooms. In Shakespeare, whenever you go into the country you're going into an anarchic territory where social structures don't apply or where they are radically renegotiated. *Anything* can happen there.

Our Arden didn't have trees or logs. It had mirrors, a clock that didn't tick – because time is suspended there – and swags of white silk that could be used in many ways, to create many images. It was a place that allowed for chaos.

Arden stands in contrast to the Court, 'the world of order, such as it is'.

'Order' is only a thin veneer covering the most chaotic and volatile of realities. The Court is structured around traditionally male values, it's a patriarchy established on masculine priorities. It's all suggested in Orlando's story: Orlando is the younger brother kept 'rustically at home' by his bad brother Oliver, who treats him like a menial and allows him neither education, dignity nor freedom. Orlando's complaint about this situation opens the play; he tells the old servant Adam that he's reached the end of his endurance and he wants out. He's taking the archetypal male exit, he's going off to Court to challenge the Duke's wrestler, to try to win fame and a name.

The Court is a place where the idea of having a good time is to watch blood sports, to watch two men bashing the life out of each other. The wrestling sequence (I, ii) suggests the violence that characterises many of the relationships in the first part, the 'Court half' of the play: violence between Oliver and Orlando, violence between the Duke and Rosalind when he banishes her, violence when Celia and Rosalind, and later Orlando, are forced to flee.

The Court is the 'ordered' world. The world as we know it. The world we can identify with and recognise. But Arden: Arden is almost like the projected imagination, where it's even possible to make the most anarchic leap of all, and change your gender. Of course, Rosalind *doesn't* change gender. She doesn't become a man, but she plays the role of a man, and nobody challenges her in that; and by passing for a man, she discovers all those areas of herself that she'd never have been able to make contact with in the ordered and civilised world as a woman.

I don't think she knows she has any of what she discovers in herself *before* she finds it in Arden. But I think she has the most profound yearning. At Court she has no position. Her father has been deposed and banished; she's been deposed too – she is no longer the Duke's daughter, merely his niece. She's there on sufferance. And I think the play starts with Rosalind in a state of overwhelming longing. She often leaves a thought uncompleted; her lines hint at feelings buried rather than expressed. She's a creature adrift.

The production's opening sequence 'placed' this nostalgia – not just Rosalind's nostalgia for a banished father but the play's nostalgia for a banished past, an 'antique world when service sweat for duty, not for need'. The stage was covered with dust-sheets thrown over abandoned furniture. The costumes were modern – Rosalind and Celia might have stepped out of that month's *Vogue*, Orlando wore army-surplus gear – but they made the same point, for in 1985 fashion was itself nostalgic, with everyone looking as if they belonged to a former age.
    The opening scene – Orlando complaining to Adam, then Oliver persuading Charles, the Duke's wrestler, to break his brother's neck – was staged like a front-of-cloth scene. It was set against a billowing grey curtain that looked like a storm cloud. A blast of wind gusted it away, revealing a 'memory place': an attic, perhaps, or a long-redundant nursery.
    Rosalind entered running, then stopped, as if hit by a wave of pain. Ludicrously out of place in an evening gown, she wandered among the packing crates and suitcases. She tugged on a dust-sheet. It fell away. Underneath was a mirror. Slowly, she wound herself in the cloth, watching her reflection in the mirror. Behind her a grandfather clock stood silent in the corner. Then Celia entered. She was clutching a champagne bottle by the scruff of its neck, stalking her cousin. Having run her to ground, she finally spoke the first words of the scene, growling them: 'I pray thee, Rosalind, sweet my coz, *be merry.*'
    Initially Juliet liked the images that were being invented in the speechless prologue to Shakespeare's scene. Later, though, she came to see their limitations.

They established the idea that the play starts not at the beginning of something, but with Rosalind nearing the *end* of her endurance. It's as if she'd been sitting at some state banquet, and it came time for the brandy and speeches, and somebody stood up to toast 'the duke', and Rosalind, suddenly no longer able to bear the usurpation and the loss, had had to get out. So she ran away to that attic, to touch her father's things. That image showed a Rosalind rooted to the past, unable to *move* because her only relationship is with the past.

It was a good idea to set that scene in a place where Rosalind and Celia felt free to talk to each other, where they could escape from the extremely oppressive male world of the Court to their own planet, like children in a tree-house who develop a kind of culture with each other, a private language that is their escape. They do just that later in the scene, when they devise 'sports' that are word games.

But the place we had invented encouraged us to be too pensive; that languid opening sequence – lifting lids, looking at old pictures – was in danger of depriving the scene of the energy Shakespeare built into it. The 'attic-ness' of it dominated the rhythm of the first part of the scene. But the scene isn't just about depression or melancholia. It's also about volatility, feverishness, swiftness of thought and of mood change. The dynamic energy starts with Celia's imperative: 'Be merry!' and Rosalind bursts back with, 'I show more mirth than I am mistress of.'

I think Shakespeare intended the actors to come on together, in the middle of an exchange. If you've been wandering around a set picking up clothes out of trunks and acting melancholy, you can't then play a scene with the same dynamic as if you'd walked on together arguing.

And that's what Shakespeare's written. We learned after we'd been playing it for a few months that you are better off if you observe the clues he gives you. The scene is a direct counterpart, a mirror, to Orlando's opening scene. Orlando starts the play at full tilt: 'As I remember, Adam, it was upon this fashion . . .' Boom, you're in there, straight away; he careers through his history in top gear, telling you exactly what his reality is and culminating with, 'I will no longer endure it!' That's his first speech. And Rosalind, dynamically, should be doing the same thing.

If you make a decision to impose a stage image on Shakespeare's language – there is a trend towards a dependence on the visual image at the expense of the verbal imagery created by the language – or if production choices set a different rhythm to the one the language is setting, you may be creating trouble for yourselves.

Celia had to stimulate the action to the energy level required by the lines. Fiona Shaw thought of her champagne bottle as 'the gear stick that shifted the scene out of neutral. It was to do with *fun*, with trying to be free in a terribly tight world.' But it was also to do with establishing a different rhythm for the scene so that, she points out, her Celia could speak her first speech.

> Herein I see thou lovest me not with the full weight
> that I love thee. If my uncle, thy banished father, had
> banished thy uncle, the duke my father . . .

has a rhythm to it that cannot be full of the lethargic invented
'prologue' rhythm. It's staccato, it has an incredibly charming
formality, all balances and counterbalances and antitheses. It tells
you who Celia is: she's a character who has a desire to say things
pertinently and yet delicately. She doesn't say, 'I love you'. Because
she is Celia, she says 'I love you' in a way which allows for a hint of
slight separation from things, and the possibility of irony, as though
she would like to connect with her feeling, but it is so passionate she
dares not.

Juliet saw Rosalind, by contrast, as 'very inaccessible at the beginning of
the play'.

She seems to be very private in her utterances. Indeed, except when
alone with Celia, she hardly speaks at all: and the fact that she
doesn't speak has to be focused upon, her very silence has to be given
space. Her distraction, her speechlessness, her lack of centre have to
be *placed*, because out of that come all her choices in the second half
of the play.

Celia and Rosalind's enclosed, private world was violently interrupted
when the attic suddenly filled with men, limbering up for the wrestling
match that was to be played before the Court. The Duke, in military
evening dress, carried a brandy snifter and briefly kissed his daughter;
his courtiers brought in the atmosphere of a gentlemen's club. The
women seemed suddenly out of place, uneasy. Orlando, hunched in an
army-surplus greatcoat, was equally 'wrong', conspicuously David to
Charles the Wrestler's Goliath. But when Celia and Rosalind hesitantly
stepped forward to urge him not to fight, Orlando gently silenced
them: this was his only chance. Juliet saw in the wrestling another
mirror of Rosalind's predicament:

Orlando has been in the same 'I won't endure it' situation as
Rosalind, but here he takes the almost parodic male way out of it.
He fights. But Rosalind, too, is engaged in a kind of struggle, and
when she offers all 'the little strength that I have' – every cell of my
body is yours, fight for us both – she seems to be recognising
something in his desperate challenge that is like her own. The

wrestling is a very primal image, and it's a catalyst, it serves as a release for everyone who watches it. My feeling was that if it hadn't been for the wrestling, Rosalind might never have found the energy to get out of the Court. I interpret 'love at first sight' as Rosalind recognising something in Orlando, maybe a history like her own, maybe a reflection of herself.

The wrestling ends in a fairy-tale triumph for Orlando, but when the Duke learns he is the son of one of the courtiers who supported the deposed Duke, he spurns him. Relationships stiffen. 'We've all been speaking prose for the whole play so far,' says Juliet. 'Now we lock into verse.' The Duke storms out. The women edge forward. Celia offers solace. Rosalind seizes the opportunity and, in her most overt gesture so far, gives Orlando a token. He is too smitten to respond but she 'hears' silent Orlando call them back when they turn to leave.

In the next scene (I, iii) the Duke returns, furious at Orlando's impudence, suspicious of his niece. He banishes Rosalind: 'Get you from our court.' Juliet spoke Rosalind's gasp of surprise, 'Me, uncle?' as if she'd been hit in the solar plexus.

But with Rosalind, the more turbulent the inner experience, the more she contains it in the formal structure of the verse. Her thought is like a rope that she's climbing hand over hand. She's not silenced by his threat of 'Get out or die.' She takes a breath and responds, 'Let me the knowledge of my fault bear with me' – not, 'Don't banish me,' but 'Tell me why.' She doesn't implore, she challenges. It arrests him. And now she takes a bigger breath:

> If with myself I hold intelligence
> Or have acquaintance with mine own desires,
> If that I do not dream or be not frantic –
> As I do trust I am not – then, dear uncle,
> Never so much as in a thought unborn
> Did I offend your highness.

She demonstrates such control. She sustains a perfectly regular metre through those lines, holding on to a rhythm which is fluid, rational and calm: 'if, if, or, or, as, *then*'. It is empowering her, harnessing that power to lend fuller authority to 'Never . . ./Did I offend your highness.' Instead of being fragmented by this ex-perience she begins to collect her sense of self. As with many of Shakespeare's women, adverse experience makes Rosalind self-determining, it restores her tenacity. She *knows* that what the Duke is saying makes no sense: she is no traitor.

Celia recovers the scene when the Duke strides out again. She collects her bewildered cousin and, balanced line upon balanced line, still holding emotion at arm's length, suggests the staggering plan to elope. Rosalind laughs and comes up with her first 'initiating' idea: she will dress up as a man – a 'swashing and a martial' man: a Ganymede. 'A startled look crossed Celia's face,' says Fiona, 'but then it was too late!' They were on their way to Arden, and in Arden the balance of their friendship would radically shift. Fiona identifies in this shifting balance a tension between Celia and Rosalind that challenges the actresses who play the roles, for, in the first act, *As You Like It* looks like Celia's play. Celia initiates all the action and makes all the decisions: to watch the wrestling, to try to persuade Orlando not to fight, to comfort him, to lead Rosalind into Arden to find the banished Duke, to love unreservedly:

> thou and I am one.
> Shall we be sundered? Shall we part, sweet girl?
> No, let my father seek another heir . . .
> Say what thou canst, I'll go along with thee.

'But that,' says Fiona, 'is the end of Celia's play! Once they get to Arden, Celia's just a spectator. All that initiative – in Arden, Celia's silent!' Rosalind's play is just the opposite: observer at Court, initiator in Arden. Actresses who play the roles have to negotiate room for each other. Fiona again:

Juliet decided – sometimes, she thought, rashly – to relinquish the beginning of the play to me, and to let Celia run it. That made life difficult for her, having to establish a silent, reticent Rosalind with the audience. I in turn felt that Celia needed the focus in the first part in order to render up with grace the second half. Juliet and I became friends. The only way to do this play was to do it together.

In some ways Arden looked just like the Court, for Arden was through the looking glass – the looking glass that had been on stage since Rosalind uncovered it. Now its surface rolled down and Celia's father, the Duke, wrapped in a white dust-sheet, stepped through the empty frame to become Rosalind's father, the banished Duke. The same courtiers who had watched the wrestling pulled dust-covers over their shoulders and became his 'co-mates in exile'.

The new exiles – Rosalind, Celia and the Court fool, Touchstone – arrived in Arden carrying winter on their backs, tugging long coils of white parachute silk pulled from the centre of a frozen moon that spread out to cover everything as they trudged. Celia, not dressed for snow, collapsed exhausted, while Touchstone, in top hat, set down his luggage – a carefully tied box of cigars – and Rosalind, in pin stripes and overcoat, her hair cropped, announced, 'So this is the forest of Arden.' The wild discrepancy between expectation and reality made the scene wonderfully funny. Fiona's Celia

just sat there thinking, 'This is terrible. *Awful.*' She's frozen, miserable. She'd packed her diamond necklaces in I, iii: 'Let's away/And get our jewels and our wealth together.' What the hell is she going to do with jewels in the forest? Nobody's brought the sandwiches. Celia had no idea what she'd let herself in for! And then slowly, slowly, Rosalind comes into her own.

From now on, of course, it is Ganymede everyone in Arden sees, not Rosalind, but for Juliet there was a constant tension between her character and her disguise. Ganymede did not simply replace Rosalind in Arden: he ran parallel with her. The two would sometimes collude, sometimes collide and even sometimes betray each other. To begin with, Juliet discovered, the disguise forced Rosalind to flex muscles she didn't know she had.

She arrives in Arden saying she could 'cry like a woman', but she then realises that because she's dressed as a boy, certain things are expected of her. So she has to fulfil them. Then she finds she can, and a kind of courage is born in her that's never been asked of her before. She buys a house. There's a muscle exercised for the first time! She employs a servant – another muscle exercised. Her disguise sets her on a voyage of discovery. What else might she discover she can do?

Literally and figuratively the disguise releases her: you have to imagine her going into doublet and hose from Elizabethan petticoat and farthingale and a rib-cracking corset. To get out of that corset must be such a relief! (In fact I know it's a relief: I loved getting out of that *Vogue* gown into trousers, having tottered around in tight skirts and heels for the first hour.) Rosalind can stretch her limbs, she can breathe properly, and so she's able to embark on increasingly long sweeps of thought and expression that take her ever deeper into new terrain.

And in this production Orlando, in so many ways Rosalind's mirror image, explored his female nature. He arrives in Arden carrying old Adam in his arms like a child, picturing himself as a 'doe', the frail old man his 'fawn'.

Gender roles are turned on their heads here. Orlando plays the conventional woman's part in the play. He doesn't initiate any of the action of *As You Like It* (except at the very end). He isn't the pivot or the motor of the play. He's there entirely in relation to Rosalind; his role as her lover is his identity. He spends most of his time asking questions – which she answers – and what happens to him is classically what happens to women in Shakespeare. His love is tested. Rosalind/Ganymede uproots his idea of the wooing process. Not only is Orlando being wooed, not wooing, but his hopelessly romantic notions of wooing are deconstructed in the process.

Rosalind's wooing games took place in an Arden transformed by time. After the interval Arden had greened. The clock and mirror were still there, cased in green. A natural mirror, a stream, crossed the stage. The parachute silk that had created winter hung high over centre stage, now a symbolist copse. Each of the characters who entered this transformed scene was changed, too: Orlando spring-heeled and barefoot; Rosalind apt for clowning in Chaplin trousers; Celia wrapped in something like a picnic table-cloth that meant she didn't need to cross her ankles any more.

The games begin in III, ii when Orlando's love verses are discovered impaled on every unlikely surface. Celia, oblivious to Rosalind's presence, comes on reading one aloud.

She's reading, 'Why should this a desert be?', trying to make head or tail of this ridiculous poem. My Celia, who had a relationship to language, also had an intellectual snobbery about it that was wonderfully displayed at this moment. Celia recognises trite verse when she sees it. And this is *trite* verse. Trite *love* verse. Celia is someone who, in Act I, reacted to love as if she'd been presented with a smelly sock. Love is to be disdained. And trite verse reinforces her opinion.

Rosalind doesn't know the author of the verse; Celia does, and Fiona's sceptical reading of the poem released a complex of emotions. The love expressed in the poem was dangerous. Celia sensed a friendship on the point of disintegration, but she wouldn't let Rosalind go without a fight. Her irony lampooned what would shortly knock the wind out of Rosalind. To good effect: it got Rosalind laughing at idealised love, so that when Orlando appears it isn't knee-trembling Rosalind but anti-romantic Ganymede who steps out of hiding to meet him. As Juliet puts it,

she tries to 'speak to him like a saucy lackey': 'Do you hear, forester?' When Orlando replies, 'Very well. What would you?' she's stumped. What does she want that she can express in disguise? Erm . . . 'I pray you, what is't o'clock?' She might as well have said, 'Got a light?' It's that witless. She hasn't a clue what she's going to say to him so she says the most banal thing in the world. He responds, 'There's no clock in the forest.' Undaunted, she then launches into a dazzling performance. 'I'll tell you who Time ambles withal, who Time trots withal . . .' Once again, the arcs of her language get longer and longer until you almost have to draw air into your boots to get through it. At the beginning of the scene the breath is coming in shallow gulps – the delirium, the nerves, the shock, the anticipation show up in the breathing. But then as things develop, the breath gets deeper and deeper as she grows more confident with what she's discovering.

This Time speech isn't just decorative, isn't just a *tour de force*. Yes, she is showing off. She is displaying like a peacock to get his attention, and it's hardly surprising that she does it by using her agility with language, since that's her proven resource and since here conceptualised thought is both a stimulant and a protection. She's a mental dancer. She's thinking on her feet. And she moves so fast, all he can do is ask the questions.

But it's more than that because, having grabbed his attention, she then launches into parody. She's gaining confidence in the role she is playing as Ganymede, and it leads her to people her conceit with other characters – the priest who lacks Latin, the rich man without gout, the condemned thief, the idle lawyer. Rosalind was performing as Ganymede, now Ganymede starts performing!

Her capacity to play all roles and to manipulate her own disguise successfully is potentially a danger to Rosalind: Rosalind might have so interesting a time as Ganymede that she's unable to commit herself to Rosalind again. Yet it's Rosalind, not Ganymede, whom Orlando requires – and the happy ending requires – at the close of the play.

For the time being, though, a curious double-act between Rosalind and

Ganymede played out the rest of this scene, mocking Orlando, scorning love, proposing the cure, setting up the ultimate role-play, in which Orlando must 'imagine me his love . . . call me "Rosalind" and come every day to my cote, and woo me'. Which of them was it, at the end of the scene, who turned artlessly to Celia to say, 'Come, sister, will you go?' Fiona heard Rosalind speak the line, and she was 'appalled'. It made their next scene a sore trial of friendship.

Orlando had agreed to the wooing game but stood Ganymede up in III, iv. Rosalind was racked with disappointment and Celia, says Fiona, was 'finding it very difficult to find a way of negotiating around her friend, who is being impossible'. Denied the wooing scene she expected, the play gives Rosalind a surrogate. In another part of the forest, other lovers are engaged in other wooing games. As Juliet sees it, 'Shakespeare is building the play out of a series of duologues on the nature of love, and the play is going to show us lots of versions that don't work.' Rosalind and Celia eavesdrop on one of them: they listen as the love-sick shepherd Silvius tries in vain to soften the heart of scornful Phebe. Rosalind/Ganymede restrains herself for a while but suddenly explodes into their drama:

I think Ganymede strides into the scene with that diatribe at Phebe – 'Who might be your mother?' – because Rosalind is so outraged by the roles Silvius and Phebe are playing out. In this love duet we see, in Silvius, love of the aesthetic kind, as it appears in hyperbolic love poetry. He is a kind of earnest Durham graduate with a penchant for complaint literature. He's placing Phebe on a pedestal, and Rosalind has to make him see how destructive that is. Some forms of love *are* destructive. Iconoclastically, Rosalind keeps chipping away at the pedestal he's erected.

Silvius is in love with the idea of love, and with his role as the jilted lover, and Phebe is in love with *being* loved without learning to return it. Most of Phebe's imagery has to do with pain, with inflicting hurt – 'executioner', 'murderer', 'butchers', 'wound', 'scratch', 'scar', and although she repudiates the effect of the imagery as she uses it, I think what that's doing is revealing someone incapable of love because she doesn't love herself. I think it would be interesting to see Phebe played as a person who is damaged in some way – someone obsessed with the outer because she can't deal with the inner. The world is full of women like that.

What Rosalind is trying to make Silvius see is that he perpetuates Phebe's cruelty, her image of herself. Rosalind is saying, 'If you put her up on a pedestal, she will behave as if she's sixty feet in the air above you, so don't then be surprised if she shits on your head like a pigeon.'

But she is also discovering pragmatism in love. 'I see no more in you/Than without candle may go dark to bed'; 'Sell when you can, you are not for all markets.' They're very funny, those lines, but they're saying something very serious too.

Rosalind may be on the attack in this scene but Ganymede is under attack. Rosalind becomes uncomfortably aware that Phebe is falling in love with Ganymede. 'What means this? Why do you look on me?' she asks as Phebe ogles Ganymede. "Od's my little life, I think she means to tangle my eyes too!' In that instant, Rosalind made a discovery. Deciding to wear trousers, to role-play a fictional man, was going to have actual repercussions: a girl had just fallen in love with her disguise!

Rosalind may be the catalyst for the anarchy of the play, but whatever chaos she causes, she's going to be responsible for it. So Rosalind is brought back to earth by the scene. Celia is creasing herself with laughter. And those sharp edges of love, the ones suggested by the love of Celia for Rosalind, become reality with Phebe loving Ganymede.

As happens in so many of the scenes in this play, the character who starts out exposing others is herself exposed. Rosalind is not by any means in control. Every time she discovers one answer, that answer throws up more questions. Each collision with each new character shears a new facet on to the prism of love.

That word 'collision' is very apt. Because by now As You Like It is looking like a game of billiards and the Forest of Arden like Clapham Junction. Every character collides with every other character and each incident yields some new revelation about love which builds up into the play's joyful vision.

Finally, having dispatched everyone else's love affairs, Rosalind gets back to her own. Orlando at last appears in IV, i and she lambasts him.

The teacher has been waiting for her pupil to show up: Ganymede is supposed to be giving a wooing lesson. But the woman in love has been waiting too, and that woman is very vulnerable, very exposed. Rosalind, unlike the audience, doesn't know the end of the play. Orlando may never show up! By now she's spent most of the play talking to other people. There's the scariness of having tipped herself into love with someone, and, having tumbled, it can be terrifying.

And yet, fortunately, she has this structure, this Ganymede, to make it possible to deal with the chaos of feeling that's overwhelming her. Ganymede affords her the control that might otherwise be beyond her. That is not to say that the 'man' Rosalind can control things the 'woman' can't. Because it's always only Rosalind. It's just that the disguise, and the perceived role imposed upon her by the disguise, force her to detach just sufficiently to be able to free the mind from the trammels of the heart. What she's experiencing emotionally is very real, but she's channelling it, through role-play, into something controllable. And that way she doesn't expose too much. She doesn't do too much damage. She can quickly and lightly restore the scene to harmony. And she can use this structure to explore Orlando's response.

I'll tell you what it's like: it's like acting. You go on stage and you're two people: you are yourself, the actress, but you are also a character; you are bound by the dictates of playing somebody else within a fiction, a piece of make-believe. So you may be feeling all manner of things about what a fellow actor is doing, but you don't have the means in the fiction to express that. What you do have at your disposal, as the actress, is a variety of choices by which you can make those feelings manifest, without destroying the fiction.

What is wonderful about the beginning of the wooing scene is the scale of the chastisement. The scale of her thought is always commensurate with the rhythms of her language. And it's very funny. Because it's a completely over-the-top reaction. I don't think Orlando had a clue. I think he thought it was going to be really charming, wooing games under cherry blossoms, and what does he get? The biggest roasting of his life! Rosalind rails at him, tears him to shreds, rages. She will not let him off the hook. She's a love guerrilla!

> Break an hour's promise in love? He that will divide a minute into a thousand parts, and break but a part of the thousandth part of a minute in the affairs of love, it may be said of him that Cupid hath clapped him o'th'shoulder, but I'll warrant him heart-whole.

It has the protection and qualification of role-play, but it isn't a spoof. Rosalind isn't burlesquing some archetype of female behaviour in love, she's not sending up the idea that women in love are volatile, difficult. Women *are* volatile in love – whether we approve of it or not, we are. She is allowing him to see the complexity, the perversity, the contradictions he will find inherent in female nature. The object is not to expose those contradictions so he can avoid them or get rid of them, it's so he can take them on board, because they are inevitably going to be there. Those contradictions are going to be a part of his future.

What is also glorious is that this is the scene when Rosalind is able to play Rosalind, because now the conceit is in place, that she will play a woman. So for the first time since she put the trousers on Rosalind can directly use her own responses. She doesn't have to conceal them because she has the role-play as a framework inside which she can be herself. And she's there with this person she's madly in love with, basking in mutual discovery, but always having a safety catch on the door.

They give each other such energy in the scene. And they go on such a long journey together. She discovers as she goes along, as she tests him, as she explores his reactions again and again, that the lettering goes all the way through the rock: Orlando is the real thing.

But she is also discovering and testing herself. She isn't a know-all; if she becomes knowing, she becomes closed. I don't think she *knows* any more about love than Orlando does. But, being a woman, her relationship to it is different. Perhaps because she knows what it costs. It can cost women their lives. And for some reason she has that knowledge: she knows that right from the start of the play. The stakes are often higher for women. But the reality of loving is as new for her as for him – it's just that because she plays the role of teacher, she has to articulate the discoveries.

The centre of Rosalind's instruction is surely this: Orlando, ready to die for love, should 'die by attorney', since in all six thousand years of the world's history no man has 'died in his own person, videlicet, in a love cause': 'men have died from time to time, and worms have eaten them, but not for love.' Juliet's director thought the line should be played sorrowfully, a mournful reflection that romantic love is merely a posture. But Juliet couldn't agree.

It was one of those examples when you find in a rehearsal room that the male and female experience of loving are in some ways different. It was difficult to compromise. Either I played it Adrian's way, against what I felt to be my own experience, or I played it my way and denied him his interpretation, his experience. In the end I chose my own interpretation: Rosalind isn't *regretting* that romanticism doesn't exist; she is debunking the whole myth of romanticism, and saying, 'These romantic myths persist, but they are lies.' She's being iconoclastic again.

That scene with Phebe shows what happens when you put women on a pedestal. It can't be in any woman's interest to be the object of idealised love, because the same instinct that elevates her this week may well dump her in the gutter next week. Contrary to all those conventions in pulp romance magazines, it is often men, not women, who are the conservers of romantic idealism, and who then rewrite history to authorise these distorted perceptions.

It's so modern, it's what the feminist movement has been doing for the past twenty-odd years, taking sacredly held myths and beginning to prise them open. And 'open' is the operative word, because Rosalind's iconoclasm isn't destructive, she isn't just wantonly smashing Orlando's illusions, she's breaking through a carapace of expectation and prejudgement to liberate the woman – warts and all. Rosalind is telling Orlando that it is of no use to women if men do not see the warts. Women have to be allowed their fallibility, their flaws, their humanness; and that's a process of opening up, for both men and women.

(What Rosalind has to say is also very funny. Troilus didn't die for Cressida, he had 'his brains dashed out with a Grecian club'; Leander didn't die for Hero, he was 'taken with a cramp and drowned'. Her revisionist obituaries are so deeply unglamorous!)

Orlando is attentive to this astonishing lesson, yet Juliet thinks his appalled response teaches Rosalind something:

Rosalind is at her most acerbic, her most percipient, her wittiest in these exchanges, but Orlando's reaction, 'I would not have my right Rosalind of this mind, for I protest her frown might kill me,' utterly disarms her. Orlando somehow doesn't seem to have absorbed the content of her speech quite yet. But she doesn't reject him. She replies with one of the tenderest lines of the play, which isn't repealing her former statement but is making space for something quite different from that witty alienation. She says, 'By this hand, it will not kill a fly.' Love breathes through those open vowels! It's so wonderfully gentle.

That moment of repose seems almost to recharge Rosalind. 'Come,' she commands, 'ask me what you will,' and then she bounds away,

'like a gazelle,' says Juliet. She's more outrageously subversive even as she's recklessly orthodox. On the one hand she vows to love Orlando *and* 'twenty such', raising for him the spectre of promiscuity on an unimaginable scale; on the other, she turns to Celia to demand, 'Marry us'.

It's as though that first impulse puts her immediately in touch with the necessity to contain it. She has to play out the marriage ceremony because she's just raised the issue of humanity's potential for sexual excess. Human sexual appetites are not by nature monogamous! Yet they have to be controlled, especially in a place that is itself chaotic and unstructured, like Arden. That's why in the middle of the forest we have to role-play marriage. Otherwise Rosalind is in trouble. Her warning lights are flashing on and off because what she's feeling is becoming so powerful, and her appetite is growing by the minute.

Sometimes in the scene it seems that she has lost her sense of role-play. It isn't Ganymede, it's pure Rosalind speaking for a moment. Then suddenly she switches, she detaches into satire and back into the game. Those points I found were her means of catapulting herself out of a situation where she's been in danger of going beyond some boundary.

The idea that she keeps coming back to in the scene is that love must be based on knowledge. Not myth: not Leander dying for Hero's love. And not hyperbole: when Orlando protests he'll love her 'for ever and a day' Rosalind corrects him, 'Say "a day" without the "ever".'

> Men are April when they woo, December when they wed; maids are May when they are maids, but the sky changes when they are wives.

Rosalind knows that the value placed on women when they have not yet been 'possessed' may be great, but that thereafter they will be devalued, they won't retain their worth very long.

That's sobering, for both men and women. But she doesn't indulge it. Rosalind – and here's a place where she, not Ganymede, seems on top – changes gear, absolutely threatens Orlando with love:

> I will be more jealous of thee than a Barbary cock-pigeon over his hen, more clamorous than a parrot against rain, more new-fangled than an ape, more

giddy in my desires than a monkey; I will weep for
nothing, like Diana in the fountain . . .

This statement is at the very heart of the play, and at the heart of
what composes and frames Rosalind. It's deeply anti-romantic and
consciously so, for, if women are idealised by men, how can
relationships be sustained? Men will always only ever be April when
they woo, because when they woo, they won't discover who the
real woman is. So December will be along in no time. Without
knowledge, love is not real: it remains in the area of fantasy,
romance, idealism, illusion.

So this, I think, is her credo. And she uses rather gross images to
articulate it – they're not the most beautiful of the beasts, those apes
and parrots. They're harsh, ungainly, screeching, clumsy, literally
barbaric. Bestial. She's talking about women's potential for being
not of the angels but of the beasts.

Yet it's wonderful that, within the same speech, Rosalind brings
in Diana: she takes deified Woman and pulls her into the same
argument, in the same breath as those monkeys. Because, of course,
that is what she's discovering as she goes along: women have the
double capacity to be Diana and parrot. Rosalind has already shown
it. When she gave him hell at the beginning of the scene, *she* was the
clamorous parrot. So she's discovering that love can make you ugly,
that knowledge of the loved one isn't always an *improving* acqui-
sition, that mutual knowledge is not necessarily beautiful. It can
make you grasping, fearful, rapacious, or 'jealous', 'new-fangled',
'giddy'.

Juliet's observation that 'Orlando is the woman' of the wooing games,
that 'love teaches him curiosity – he asks questions all the time, which
Rosalind answers', comes into play here. He may be bewildered by this
barrage of subversiveness, he may feel battered by it. But Rosalind
doesn't ease up.

She rarely lets him settle in his thinking. He says, 'I'll love her for
ever and a day'; she says, 'No you won't.' He says, 'Rosalind won't
do that.' She says, 'Yes she will.' She keeps whittling away the
vocabulary of his expectations. Rosalind uses this scene to explore
the differences between male wisdom and female wisdom. When,
for example, she says of women, 'The wiser, the waywarder', it's
almost a riddle because those words 'wise' and 'wayward' resonate
so differently for men and women, and Orlando takes them for

antitheses, whereas Rosalind sees them as somehow synonymous. She goes on:

> Make the doors upon a woman's wit and it will out at the casement; shut that, and 'twill out at the key-hole; stop that, 'twill fly with the smoke out at the chimney.

She's saying many things there, all of them potentially subversive. She is saying, women will not submit to your expectations of them. We will get out at key-holes, or casements, or chimneys: those apertures are quite specific and very differently shaped, but we will change our shape, like some sort of strange Protean beast, and we will get out because we are more resourceful than you may imagine.

She's also saying, 'Beware.' If you do repress us, you will have to take the consequences. You are directly responsible. Your need to contain us may manifest itself as power, but don't be fooled; your 'power' puts you in jeopardy, for if *you* create *us*, you create our waywardness too, our reactive power to find our way into our neighbour's bed. Now, you can exercise your power. But the consequences will be upon your head. Ultimately, though, the speech is very generous, because she's saying: 'Here, Orlando: this is a gift. I'm telling you that you have all the power. I'm telling you this *in time,* before the consequences arrive. The future isn't yet out of your hands.' That future is her gift.

And what does Orlando do at this point? He leaves! – saying, 'For these two hours, Rosalind, I will leave thee.' That he chooses to exit is not arbitrary. Rosalind has been flying through this scene, making incredible leaps. She's not just dancing, now, she's doing a tarantella, and suddenly he can't take it, so he says, 'I'm off.' And it renders her defenceless. 'Alas, dear love, I cannot lack thee two hours!' There's not much Ganymede in that statement . . .

Orlando leaves and now, for the first time in many minutes, the focus turns to Celia. Fiona Shaw describes Celia's point of view:

Celia sets out thinking the play is about Celia. But when she gets to Arden, she finds out that she is no Lord Hamlet, but an attendant lord in the land of love.

Her play is about a girl who went to a forest with a friend because she loved her so. But when they got there, her friend met a man and started behaving peculiarly, began to deny their friendship, became boring, apart from anything else. And started talking about love. And Celia feels she has to be there. Right in the middle of the wooing scene. She's fascinated by the conversation for voyeuristic reasons, but she senses the danger of it.

Fiona's performance was another step in a process of recuperating the role that had begun some years earlier. Sinead Cusack, who played Celia in 1982, recounts an anecdote that typifies directors' attitudes to Celia.

When Terry Hands was directing *As You* he showed us all the costume designs, which we admired. And when I looked at mine for Arden I said, 'Terry, my costume as Celia is *green*.' 'Yes,' he said. 'You haven't got a superstition about wearing green on stage, have you?' 'No, no!' 'You're Irish, aren't you?'
I said, 'Of course I'm Irish. I'm not superstitious about the colour. It's just that I'm green and so is the set. If I'm green and the set's green, I'm going to disappear into the set.' And he said, 'Don't be so stupid, Sinead. You *are* the set.'
As a result of that little exchange, I became a very obvious and determined and available Celia. I sat centre stage.

And perhaps that's exactly where Shakespeare intended her to be, an on-stage audience monitoring the wooing, interpreting it for the other audience, 'putting inverted commas around it' – Sinead's phrase. Fiona felt Shakespeare's dramaturgy to be a constant challenge:

Those scenes in Arden were written as trios, and I was determined that the trios be trios. The problem is, Celia never speaks to Orlando in these scenes. Not a word! But I still couldn't see any other way of playing them: Celia can't be there and not be there, too. Sometimes actresses solve the problem of what to do with Celia's silence by opting out, playing at falling asleep, but that drags on the energy of the scene: if the character can sleep through the scene while those lines are being spoken, why can't the audience?
I think Celia helps to focus the scene on Rosalind. Celia knows exactly what's going on, and that's very funny, because she can't do anything about it. Her face becomes a litmus paper.

Both she and Sinead felt that one of the stories Celia's plot told was 'the disintegration of a friendship, watching a friend disappear' (Fiona); 'She's leaving me; that closeness and that intimacy are going, and I don't want it to. I'm hurt' (Sinead).
For Juliet Stevenson playing Rosalind, Celia's presence, even

prominence, in her scenes was both liberating and inhibiting.

Shakespeare never puts a character on stage arbitrarily. So why is Celia there? I think it's probably Rosalind who *insists* she's there.

Celia's presence allows her to be brave. In this anarchic wooing game Rosalind is playing, Celia is a chaperone, an audience to remind her always of the role-play, and of the boundaries – things could get out of hand, and nearly do – but she also lets Rosalind be more flirtatious, more daring than she could be on her own. Celia's presence serves as a trampoline: Rosalind springs higher and higher, knowing she's got that under her. Celia knows her so well, and that keeps her in touch with herself.

Celia's reaction to the mock wedding she is coerced into performing is consternation, but it is also potentially tragic. Juliet observes this.

The wedding ceremony is terribly funny because tugging at the strange solemnity is Celia's resistance. Celia is *appalled*, and you can play 'appalled' on many levels, one of which is, 'I am certainly not going to start impersonating clergymen,' or 'I am not going to marry you because God knows what you might end up doing after the ceremony!' Or you can speak the line 'I cannot say the words' as involving far more cost to Celia than either of those alternatives, as indicating that Rosalind is going almost over the horizon. 'I cannot speak the words' because I am rendered speechless by the loss of my friend.

Fiona thought Celia saw herself as abused and betrayed by Rosalind in the wooing scene.

When Orlando leaves and Celia says, 'You have simply misused our sex' – *our sex*, not our friendship – 'in your love-prate,' she's saying that by being a man you're behaving quite alienly to your nature. She's rebuking Rosalind's expressed cynicism in the scene.

Juliet's Rosalind felt otherwise.

Celia's missed the point! Rosalind hasn't misused 'our sex', she has been celebrating it, its powers and possibilities. That exchange with Celia after Orlando exited was one of my favourite moments in the whole play: Celia can't understand because she hasn't experienced it, while Rosalind is unable to make her understand what she herself finds inexpressible.

> O coz, coz, coz, my pretty little coz, that thou didst know how many fathom deep I am in love! But it cannot be sounded: my affection hath an unknown bottom, like the Bay of Portugal.

Their conflicting reactions are very serious. Celia isn't codding it up when she accuses Rosalind of being a traitor. But Rosalind has outgrown Celia. That's why they have to separate, whether they like it or not.

And they are given separate exits, Rosalind to 'find a shadow and sigh', Celia to 'sleep', but, says Fiona, 'it is the sleep of someone who is chilly with loss.'

The play works to recover that loss in Celia's next scene. It's past two o'clock; Orlando is late again; Rosalind is fuming; and once more Silvius turns up instead, still in thrall to Phebe. He hands over her letter, beaming, and it looks as if all Rosalind's lessons have failed. Haven't any of the men learned anything? But then a stranger enters, with a tale, and a bloody handkerchief; Celia falls in love and Rosalind falls in a swoon. Juliet saw the episode as 'the beginning of the disguise cracking apart'.

When Oliver – Orlando's bad brother newly come to Arden, here transformed – tells that amazing story of how Orlando found him sleeping with the lion poised to spring upon his throat, and how he killed the lion, it's almost biblical: it takes us right back to the wrestling match, only this time Orlando's fighting for salvation, not honour. Oliver produces a blood-stained napkin and Rosalind faints: it's the first time she hasn't been able to contain herself. Her heart takes over, whether or not her head wants to continue the Ganymede game, and overrides the disguise. She literally loses control.

Ultimately, in V, ii Orlando calls the halt to the role-play. Rosalind could have postponed it indefinitely: she's having so much fun in trousers. But Orlando says, 'Stop'. It's the only action he initiates in the play. And it turns the play around. 'I can live no longer by thinking,' he says, and Rosalind replies, 'I will weary you then no longer with idle talking.'

In our production, Orlando had thrown himself down beside the stream. Rosalind came and stood behind him, so what he gazed upon was Ganymede's reflection in the water. And as he looked, Ganymede began to look more and more like Rosalind while Rosalind was speaking her 'magician' speech, which is all about transformation.

> Believe then, if you please, that I can do strange things: I have, since I was three year old, conversed with a magician . . . If you do love Rosalind so near the heart as your gesture cries it out, when your brother marries Aliena, shall you marry her . . . and it is not impossible to me, if it appear not inconvenient to you, to set her before your eyes tomorrow . . . if you will be married tomorrow, you shall; and to Rosalind, if you will.

The word 'if' here enters the play as a protagonist. 'If' makes way for miracles. 'If' relies on faith: 'if' you believe, it will happen. But 'if' is also a challenge: now is the time your deeds must match your words, and so must mine. 'If you love Rosalind,' she will appear. As Touchstone will say, 'Much virtue in "if".'

Orlando used to get more and more disturbed by what he was seeing – the image in the water was becoming too real, so he would paddle the surface, the reflection would shatter, but when he turned around and looked up, Ganymede would have disappeared.

Ganymede disappears so that Rosalind can organise the end of the play by drawing together the entire forest, 'almost,' says Juliet, 'like a goddess, or a magician'.

She's gathering people together and winding up their fates, their destinies. She organises everybody, draws from them vows to perform what they have promised. Finally, this character, who has been transforming herself more and more over the five acts of the play, leaves the stage to transform herself yet again.

And when she returns, she brings on the god.

I find it difficult to talk about the final scene because so many things are happening and some of them I find emotionally contradictory. Clearly it's a celebration. Clearly it's *miraculous*: Rosalind returns transformed from man into woman, accompanied by Hymen, the god of marriage, and it's as though her magic-making properties through the play have finally given her direct access to the gods themselves. This epiphany enacts it, and the play simply lifts off like a Boeing 707: you're no longer on the ground, there's no room here for psychological realism in your choices. Hymen isn't Corin in fancy dress. Hymen *is the god* and the scene moves into the realm of the miraculous. So it's celebratory, wonderful, joyous. The play ends in delight.

But as Rosalind, I found it hard to kick up my heels. Rosalind comes on stage with Hymen, says to her father, 'To you I give myself, for I am yours,' and to Orlando, 'To you I give myself, for I am yours.' Then she says,

> I'll have no father, if you be not he;
> I'll have no husband, if you be not he;

and then to Phebe, 'Nor ne'er wed woman, if you be not she.' And that's it. Rosalind doesn't speak again. Rosalind, The Mouth, who has talked non-stop for the past three hours, is silent. And Celia stopped talking at the end of Act IV! Having met and fallen in love with Oliver, and having invited him home to the sheepcote, 'Good sir, go with us,' *she* is given nothing more to say.

You can argue that Celia and Rosalind don't have to say anything more. That Rosalind can give herself away with complete confidence and knowledge: she knows her love, she knows her lover (and she knows herself). She's said everything she has to say. So she can give everything away without loss and without damage.

But you can argue, too, that they are silent for the same reason that they fell silent in Act I when the Court invaded their attic: that the patriarchy is reasserting itself. A male god dispenses marriage: 'You and you no cross shall part;/You and you are heart in heart.' You can read that as magically cohering; but you might read these slight aphorisms the god comes up with as impossibly trite.

The god descends. The Duke takes over. And then the Court reasserts itself. It literally arrives back on stage: in comes someone saying, 'I am the second son of old Sir Rowland/That bring these tidings . . .' and then he proceeds to announce that the bad Duke is here, he's in the forest, and has been 'converted' – another transformation. And so the exiled Duke is restored to his position as the figure of ultimate authority and the hierarchies of the structured world re-emerge.

So Celia and Rosalind are now married, and are to return to the place where they first came from. They will take the experience of Arden with them. They will live in the 'reality' of Arden, with the knowledge, the exploration and the questions that Arden allowed them, but they are nevertheless going back, and the real world is now the unknown quantity as that Arden once was.

In our production what happened was that Jaques, who refuses to join in the celebration, who banishes himself to the Duke's 'abandoned cave', stepped back through the looking glass. And then the grandfather clock started ticking. 'Real' time reasserted itself.

What about the very end of the play? What did Juliet feel about the final stage picture?

Shakespeare finishes the play with a dance. There seems to be no room left for words now. All the language is pooled into this dynamic ritualising of order. But what kind of dance should it be? What do we want to say at the end of this play? Decisions about how to choreograph the dance throw up all the questions the play has explored, so I argued that we couldn't have choreography which simply enacted conventional gender roles – the men strong and butch and doing a lot of lifting, and the women helpless and decorative, flopping around in the men's arms. Having spent three hours challenging notions of gender, we couldn't then end with a final stage picture which was clichéd and stereotypical, which threw the whole play away. Adrian did point out to me that, whether I liked it or not, Shakespeare was a monarchist, a reactionary, a bourgeois and a conservative, but I said, 'I think it's irrelevant what Shakespeare was. The fact is the *play* asks the most anarchic questions. It doesn't attempt to resolve them, so why should we?'

I don't think Shakespeare's plays ever attempt to answer questions. They *ask* questions, and they leave those question marks hanging over the heads of the actors and the audience at the end of the play. That's when the audience's work starts, because they have to go home with those questions unanswered. What directors often like to do is to send the audience home with a package which has done the work for them – brought those questions to a point where they are somehow answerable, and then answered them – usually by celebrating the very status quo which the play has set out to challenge.

As You Like It ends when the argument of the play reaches a certain conclusion, but not when things are resolved. Shakespeare seems to be saying, 'Right, it's time these characters went back to the real world, and took these discoveries with them.'

At the end, the characters of the play and the people in the auditorium are faced with the same questions, the same challenges. Both actors and audience have to stop messing about in the land of possibility, to go back to the land of practical reality, to leave the theatre, to go home – hope you don't get mugged! – and, after a rather short night's sleep, get up and go to work in the morning.

But if you've allowed the play to work on you, to inform you at all, you are slightly different from when you went into the theatre. And how are you going to allow that to affect your existence? If plays can help people to deal with what life delivers them, I think they are fulfilling their role. That's why the theatre is as important as the chemist or the baker, and why every town should have one.

I don't expect audiences to go skipping out of *As You Like It* humming the tunes, because the play isn't about that. It isn't about confirming cosy opinions or settled stereotypes. It isn't about a woman in search of romantic love. The search is for knowledge and for faith, and in that search Rosalind is clamorous – as clamorous as 'a parrot against rain'!

I would hope that the audience go out of the theatre talking to each other. Wouldn't it be good? Talking to each other, maybe even ringing each other up over the next week or two?

List of Productions

Katherine Paola Dionisotti
Bianca Zoë Wanamaker
Petruchio Jonathan Pryce
Lucentio Anthony Higgins
Grumio David Suchet
Tranio Ian Charleson
Baptista Paul Brooke
Curtis Juliet Stevenson

Directed by Michael Bogdanov
Designed by Chris Dyer

First performance 7 October 1982

Katherine Sinead Cusack
Bianca Alice Krige
Petruchio Alun Armstrong
Lucentio Mark Rylance
Grumio Pete Postlethwaite
Tranio John Bowe
Baptista David Waller
Curtis William Haden
Christopher Sly Geoffrey Freshwater

Directed by Michael Bogdanov
Designed by Bob Crowley

First performance 3 September 1987

Katherine Fiona Shaw
Bianca Felicity Dean
Petruchio Brian Cox
Lucentio Alex Jennings
Grumio Barrie Rutter
Tranio Bruce Alexander
Baptista George Raistrick
Curtis Derek Hutchinson

Directed by Jonathan Miller
Designed by Stefanos Lazaridis
Costumes by Martin Chitty

2
Measure for Measure

First performance 21 June 1978

Isabella Paola Dionisotti
Mariana Marjorie Bland
Mistress Overdone Darlene Johnson
Duke of Vienna Michael Pennington
Angelo Jonathan Pryce
Escalus Raymond Westwell
Claudio Allan Hendrick
Lucio John Nettles
Provost Donald Douglas
Pompey Richard Griffiths
Whores and Nuns Susanna Bishop
Juliet Stevenson
Ruby Wax

Directed by Barry Kyle
Designed by Christopher Morley

First performance 29 September 1983

Isabella Juliet Stevenson
Mariana Emma Watson
Mistress Overdone Peggy Mount
Duke of Vienna Daniel Massey
Angelo David Schofield
Escalus Joseph O'Conor
Claudio Paul Mooney
Lucio Richard O'Callaghan
Provost Oliver Ford Davis
Pompey Anthony O'Donnell

Directed by Adrian Noble
Designed by Bob Crowley

3
Macbeth

First performance 6 November 1986

Lady Macbeth Sinead Cusack
Lady Macduff Pennie Downie
Witches Dilys Lane
Susan Porrett
Joely Richardson
Macbeth Jonathan Pryce
Duncan Alfred Burke
Banquo Hugh Quarshie
Macduff Peter Guinness
Porter David Troughton

Directed by Adrian Noble
Designed by Bob Crowley

4
All's Well That Ends Well

First performance 11 November 1981

Helena	Harriet Walter
Countess of Rossillion	Dame Peggy Ashcroft
Widow	Gillian Webb
Diana	Cheryl Campbell
Bertram	Mike Gwilym
Parolles	Stephen Moore
Lavache	Geoffrey Hutchings
King of France	John Franklyn-Robbins
Lafeu	Robert Eddison
Directed by	Trevor Nunn
Designed by	John Gunter
Costumes by	Lindy Hemming

4
Cymbeline

First performance 4 November 1987

Imogen	Harriet Walter
The Queen	Julie Legrand
Posthumus	Nicholas Farrell
Cymbeline	David Bradley
Pisanio	Jim Hooper
Cloten	Bruce Alexander
Iachimo	Donald Sumpter
Caius Lucius	Geoffrey Freshwater
Directed by	Bill Alexander
Costumes by	Allan Watkins

5
As You Like It

First performance 11 April 1985

Rosalind	Juliet Stevenson
Celia	Fiona Shaw
Phebe	Lesley Manville
Oliver	Bruce Alexander
Orlando	Hilton McRae
Duke Frederick/Senior	Joseph O'Conor
Silvius	Roger Hyamf
Directed by	Adrian Noble
Designed by	Bob Crowley

Index